LENT
for
EVERYONE
MATTHEW

YEAR A

Want to read the Bible with others?
Want to have bigger conversations around your Bible study?
Like the sound of working through this book as part of a national community?

JOIN THE BIG READ FOR LENT 2011!

Think about how deeply you'd like to be involved and choose from the following options:

- just read the book;
- download house-group study materials from http://bigbible.org.uk/resources/;
- participate in an online forum, sharing ideas and discussing Big Read themes;
- take advantage of tips, tricks, interviews and training in social media (materials can be found on social media sites; enter **#bigbible** and **#bigread2011**).

All purchasers of this book will have access to a daily newsletter from Twelve Baskets, which includes additional encouraging material.

*To access the material provided by Twelve Baskets, go to http://www.twelvebaskets. co.uk. Sign up for a free account, entering the code **bigbible12b** during the sign-up process.*

The Big Read launches with locally organized Mardi Gras suppers on 8 March 2011. Access all the materials from http://bigbible.org.uk.

The Big Bible Project is supported by the following:

LENT
for
EVERYONE

MATTHEW

YEAR A

TOM
WRIGHT

First published in Great Britain in 2011

Society for Promoting Christian Knowledge
36 Causton Street
London SW1P 4ST
www.spckpublishing.co.uk

British Library Cataloguing-in-Publication Data
A catalogue record for this book is available from the British Library

ISBN 978–0–281–06221–8

1 3 5 7 9 10 8 6 4 2

Typeset by Graphicraft Ltd, Hong Kong
Printed in Great Britain by J F Print

Produced on paper from sustainable forests

CONTENTS

CONTENTS

CONTENTS

PREFACE

———◆•◆•◆———

We called it 'the Big Read', and so it was. Thousands of people across the North-East of England, and some beyond, took part in an ecumenical project in Lent and Eastertide 2010. Luke's gospel was the book to work through that year, and so we did – in churches, in small groups involving people from several different Christian denominations, and individually. The little guidebook, *Lent for Everyone, Luke: Year C*, was designed to help people find their way through, one by one, so that they could then come together and share what they were learning.

There was great enthusiasm for the idea that we should run the project again in 2011, which is after all the four-hundredth anniversary of the King James (Authorized) Version of the Bible. There will be all kinds of Bible-related events going on in 2011, around the United Kingdom and the wider world, and we thought it was a good idea to continue the format we had used before, only this time with Matthew, the gospel set for this year.

Even though I am no longer working in the North-East, or indeed in England itself, I hope to retain a close link with this project as it moves forward, and the present little guide to Matthew is designed to that end. Once again I am very grateful to my friend and former colleague Bishop Mark Bryant for his shrewd advice and his contributions to the finished product. Once again, too, all proceeds from this book will be ploughed back into the work of God's kingdom in the North-East of

England, one of the neediest but also one of the most cheerful parts of the Church of England.

Tom Wright
University of St Andrews

ASH WEDNESDAY
Matthew 1—2; focused on 1.18–25

[18]This was how the birth of Jesus the Messiah took place. His mother, Mary, was engaged to Joseph; but before they came together she turned out to be pregnant – by the holy spirit. [19]Joseph, her husband-to-be, was an upright man. He didn't want to make a public example of her. So he decided to set the marriage aside privately. [20]But, while he was considering this, an angel of the Lord suddenly appeared to him in a dream.

'Joseph, son of David,' the angel said, 'Don't be afraid to get married to Mary. The child she is carrying is from the holy spirit. [21]She is going to have a son. You must give him the name Jesus; he is the one who will save his people from their sins.'

[22]All this happened so that what the Lord said through the prophet might be fulfilled: [23]'Look: the virgin is pregnant, and will have a son, and they shall give him the name Emmanuel,' – which means, in translation, 'God with us.'

[24]When Joseph woke up from his sleep he did what the Lord's angel had told him to. He married his wife, [25]but he didn't have sexual relations with her until after the birth of her son. And he gave him the name Jesus.

We know very, very little about Joseph. Some legends make him an old man who died while Jesus was growing up, but we don't know that for sure. We know he worked in the building trade, including what we call carpentry. We know he could trace his ancestry back to the ancient royal house of David and Solomon (many first-century Jews knew their family history as well as many today know the story of their favourite soap opera, or the fortunes of their football team). And we know that Joseph faced a unique personal and moral challenge, and came through it with integrity and humility. Joseph, in this passage, provides a sharply personal angle for us to approach Matthew's gospel.

Think how it was for him. Marriage beckons, quite likely arranged by the two families but none the less an exciting prospect. A home. Children. A new status in the community – in a small town where everyone knows everyone else and where, without television, everybody else's life is part of a complex daily soap opera.

And then the shock. Mary has news for him, news to send a chill down the spine of any prospective husband. How can he possibly believe her strange story? What will people say? So he plans, with a heavy heart, to call the whole thing off.

Then, the dream. Mary's story is true. What's more, she and her child are caught up, not just in a personal challenge, but in a much older, stranger purpose. God's purpose. God's rescue operation, long expected and at last coming true. The child to be born will be 'Emmanuel', God-with-us. God with us to save us: hence the name 'Jesus', the same word as 'Joshua', the great leader who brought the people of Israel across the Jordan into the promised land. The name means 'Yahweh saves'. God with us; God to the rescue.

Whenever God does something new, he involves people – often unlikely people, frequently surprised and alarmed people. He asks them to trust him in a new way, to put aside their natural reactions, to listen humbly for a fresh word and to act on it without knowing exactly how it's going to work out. That's what he's asking all of us to do this Lent. Reading the Bible without knowing in advance what God is going to say takes humility. Like Joseph, we may have to put our initial reactions on hold and be prepared to hear new words, to think new thoughts, and to live them out. We all come with our own questions, our own sorrows and frustrations, our own longings. God will deal with them in his own way, but he will do so as part of his own much larger and deeper purposes. Who knows what might happen, this year, if even a few of us were prepared to listen to God's word in scripture in a new way, to share the humility of Joseph, and to find ourselves caught up in God's rescue operation?

Today

Speak to us, Father, in a new way as we read your word. Help us to hear your voice and follow where you lead.

THURSDAY AFTER ASH WEDNESDAY

Matthew 3; focused on 3.1–12

[1]In those days John the Baptist appeared. He was preaching in the Judaean wilderness.

[2]'Repent!' he was saying. 'The kingdom of heaven is coming!'

[3]John, you see, is the person spoken of by Isaiah the prophet, when he said,

The voice of someone shouting in the desert:
'Prepare the route that the Lord will take,
Straighten out his paths!'

[4]John himself had clothing made from camel's hair, and a leather belt around his waist. His food was locusts and wild honey. [5]Jerusalem, and all Judaea, and the whole area around the Jordan, were going off to him. [6]They were being baptized by him in the river Jordan, confessing their sins.

[7]He saw several Pharisees and Sadducees coming to be baptized by him.

'You brood of vipers!' he said to them. 'Who warned you to escape from the coming wrath? [8]You'd better prove your repentance by bearing the right sort of fruit! [9]And you needn't start thinking to yourselves, "We have Abraham as our father." Let me tell you, God is quite capable of raising up children for Abraham from these stones! [10]The axe is already taking aim at the root of the tree. Every tree that doesn't produce good fruit is to be cut down and thrown into the fire.'

[11]'I am baptizing you with water, for repentance,' John continued. 'But the one who is coming behind me is more powerful than me! I'm not even worthy to carry his sandals. He will baptize you with the Holy Spirit and fire! [12]He's got his shovel

3

in his hand, ready to clear out his barn, and gather all his corn into the granary. But he'll burn up the chaff with a fire that will never go out.'

When a couple get married, there is so much to learn. Not so much the immediate and obvious things – favourite foods, musical tastes, good ideas for holidays, and so on. There are deeper things that make each one of us mysterious and deeply special. The rich store of memories and mental associations. The older family history: stories told and retold, sorrows quietly aching in the background, tales of an exotic cousin here, a tragic uncle there, an aunt who wrote books or a great-grandfather who was cheated in business. Such stories shape our imaginations. They condition our reactions to new situations. When you join someone else's family it takes time to learn how all this works for them. Often you can only make sense of what someone says or does up front if you get in touch with the older, deeper stories that shaped them from their earliest days.

Matthew, writing his gospel, wants to help his readers to learn the great stories of the family into which they have come through their faith in Jesus Christ. Many of his readers were probably Jewish already. That made some things easier, others harder. He is telling the story of what happened within living memory – here, the story of John the Baptist getting people ready for Jesus – but he is also helping them to get in touch with the older, deeper stories of God's ancient people. Like all early Christian writers, Matthew is eager to explain how what has happened in and through Jesus is what the ancient stories had been pointing to all along.

He's already begun to do this in the first two chapters. There's the great long family tree right at the start, of course. But there are also the times when he has pointed back to the ancient scriptures to explain the meaning of the events he's describing. Now he takes this to a new level. He picks up one of the most famous prophecies in the Old Testament, and declares that it came true in and through John the Baptist.

The prophecy in question summed up the longing and the praying of Israel over the previous five hundred years. Israel had been overrun by foreign armies. The Temple had been destroyed. God himself, they believed, had abandoned his people because of their wickedness, and had left them to their fate. Even when the Jews returned from Babylon and rebuilt the Temple, there was a lingering, uneasy sense that there was more to come, that all was not yet well. So they told the story like this: one day God will come back to rescue us. He'll come back and take charge of the whole world, and everything will be right at last. The God in heaven will be king of the earth! That's what we're waiting for.

So when John the Baptist suddenly appeared, down near the river Jordan, telling people that 'heaven' was going to take charge on earth (that's what 'the kingdom of heaven' means), it's not surprising that everyone set off to find out what was going on. John was plunging people into the Jordan. He was re-enacting the far-off moment when the ancient Israelites first entered their Promised Land. This is it! This is what we've been waiting for! Sharp-eyed people, then and later, said: This is the man the prophet spoke about. He is the 'voice in the wilderness', getting people ready for God to come back.

If we grasp nothing more than this, Matthew would have done half his job. But there are two other things going on here which also shape the way he's going to tell the rest of his story. First, lots of people coming to John have to be warned not to take God for granted. They may be Abraham's children physically, but God is doing a new thing. He is reshaping Abraham's family: sharp judgment on the one hand, an open invitation on the other. 'God is able to raise up children for Abraham from these stones!' This isn't the way many of them had been telling the story. It must have come as a shock.

Second, John kept telling people that he was preparing them for the arrival of Someone Else – Someone who would carry out this judgment against those who took their position for granted, Someone who would act in a much more dramatic way to bring the rule of 'heaven' to bear on earth. This Someone, we then discover, is Jesus himself. Everything that Matthew wants to say about Jesus must be understood as fulfilling this prophetic warning.

Those of us today who find ourselves among Jesus' followers need to pay close attention to these ancient stories. They may be strange. But only if we learn how they work will we understand what sort of a family it is we now belong to.

Today

Gracious Lord, as your heavenly rule extends on earth, help us to know your story and live as your family.

FRIDAY AFTER ASH WEDNESDAY
Matthew 4; focused on 4.18–25

[18]As Jesus was walking beside the Sea of Galilee he saw two brothers, Simon (also called Peter) and Andrew his brother. They were fishermen, and were casting nets into the sea.

[19]'Follow me!' said Jesus. 'I'll make you fish for people!'

[20]Straight away they abandoned their nets and followed him.

[21]He went on further, and saw two other brothers, James the son of Zebedee and John his brother. They were in the boat, mending their nets, with Zebedee their father. He called them. [22]At once they left the boat, and their father, and followed him.

[23]He went on through the whole of Galilee, teaching in their synagogues and proclaiming the good news of the kingdom, healing every disease and every illness among the people.

[24]Word about him went out around the whole of Syria. They brought to him all the people tormented with various kinds

of diseases and ailments, demon-possessed people, epileptics, and paralytics, and he healed them. [25]Large crowds followed him from Galilee, the Decapolis, Jerusalem, Judaea and beyond the Jordan.

There's a sense of excitement at the start of the season. The ground is prepared and marked out. The fixture list is printed. Everything is ready. So along you go for the first match.

But imagine what it would be like if, just before the game was due to start, the coach came onto the pitch and began to point to people in the stands – people who had come as spectators! 'All right: you over there, come on; and you in the blue jacket, you too; and you there hiding near the back, I want you in the team . . .' You begin to be afraid you might be next. Suddenly the people who've been called are hurrying down to the field of play, and the game begins.

Of course no serious sports team today would do it like that – or, if they did, they wouldn't win many matches. But this is the strange thing. When God came back at last, coming to establish the rule of heaven here on earth, that seems to be exactly how he went about it. Lots of people who thought they were just spectators suddenly found themselves summoned onto the field of play. As the story goes on, we find out that they, like modern spectators dragged from the stands and made to play the game, were not as ready, or as fit, as they might have been. But it seems that that's how God wanted to work.

There's something going on there which gets near the heart of the challenge of the gospel for us today. It's very easy for people to imagine that they can be 'religious' – they can say their prayers, they can go to church, they can read the Bible – but basically they are looking on, spectating, while God does whatever God is going to do. And of course there's a sense in which that's true. God is not weak, helpless, waiting for humans to get their act together before he can do anything.

But in another sense part of the point is that God always wanted humans to be part of the action, not just spectators. God made humans to reflect his image – his presence, his love, his plans – into the world. That's why he himself came into the world as a human being. And that's why Jesus called Peter, Andrew, James and John, and the others. They weren't ready. They weren't expecting it. But that's how Jesus worked then, and that's how he works to this day. Perhaps that's why you're reading Matthew's gospel right now. Perhaps Jesus is going to point to you and ask you to help him with some of the work.

Of course, there were still quite a lot of people who remained spectators. As Jesus went about healing people – which was the most dramatic way of showing them that 'heaven' really was taking charge on earth – it was natural that great crowds followed him from all over. But here's another challenge. What should the church be doing today that would make people realize that 'heaven' is actually in charge here and now? When we find the answer to that question, there will be lots more spectators – and, we may hope, lots more players too.

Today

Gracious Lord, help us to be ready when you call us to work with you.

SATURDAY AFTER ASH WEDNESDAY

Matthew 4.1–11

[1]Then Jesus was led out into the wilderness by the spirit to be tested by the devil. [2]He fasted for forty days and forty nights, and at the end of it was famished. [3]Then the tempter approached him.

'If you really are God's son,' he said, 'tell these stones to become bread!'

8

[4]"The Bible says,' replied Jesus, 'that people don't live only on bread. We live on every word that comes from God's mouth.'

[5]Then the devil took him off to the holy city, and stood him on a pinnacle of the Temple.

[6]"If you really are God's son,' he said, 'throw yourself down. The Bible does say, after all, that

God will command his angels to look after you,
and they will carry you in their hands,
so that you won't hurt your foot against a stone.'

[7]"But the Bible also says', replied Jesus, 'that you mustn't make the Lord your God prove himself!'

[8]Then the devil took him off again, this time to a very high mountain. There he showed him all the magnificent kingdoms of the world.

[9]"I'll give the whole lot to you,' he said, 'if you will fall down and worship me.'

[10]"Get out of it, satan!' replied Jesus. 'The Bible says, "Worship the Lord your God, and serve him alone!"'

[11]Then the devil left him, and angels came and looked after him.

It starts with a flicker of thought, a tiny little idea that darts across the mind while you're doing something else. It seems harmless, just one of the millions of things that the human brain comes up with. But then it returns, a minute or an hour later. You feel it now as something familiar, and perhaps enticing. If I claim travel expenses for that trip, even though I had a ride from a friend . . . if I had a chance to say that really cutting remark to the man who's always been mean to me . . . if I played my cards right, I might persuade my friend's spouse to spend an evening with me, and then maybe . . .

Always, to begin with, it seems quite reasonable, only just a bit off limits. But if we play with the idea, or allow it to play

9

with us, then a new course is set, heading for disaster at one level or another.

Christians have always found comfort in the fact that Jesus was tempted as we are. But his temptations, in this famous story, are not just an example, showing us how to resist, though of course they are that too. (Notice how his mind, well stocked with scripture, comes back again and again with the right response.) They are part of the larger story of how 'heaven's rule' came to earth.

Part of the point of the 'kingdom of heaven', you see, and of Jesus' own mission to make it happen, is that there was another power ruling the earth. If Jesus was to bring God's rescuing rule to the world, the present power had to be defeated. Jesus' 'temptations' are therefore the personal side of the larger battle he had to fight if God's rule was to take hold. Like David fighting Goliath, he had to take on the enemy one to one if the people as a whole were to be set free.

The three temptations here, like most if not all temptations, are good things that are being distorted. Bread is good. Jesus will later create a huge amount of it from a few loaves, to feed hungry people. But should he do that just for himself – and just to satisfy himself that he really is the 'Son of God', as the heavenly voice at his baptism had said? No: Jesus will satisfy himself with what God has said, rather than with any attempt to prove it.

So, too, Jesus may already have had a sense that his own vocation would end in a horrible death, trusting that God would raise him from the dead. But the satanic distortion of this is that he should perform a crazy stunt to attract attention. Again, Jesus refuses: that would be using God's power as magic.

Finally, it's clear throughout Matthew's gospel, and particularly at the very end, that Jesus as 'king of the Jews' is to become the true lord of the whole world. But the path by which he moves to that lordship is not the satanic one which would make him grab it for his own ends. The whole of the book is about the alternative path, the true way by which Jesus comes to embody heaven's rule on earth.

Once more, we are not simply spectators in this extraordinary drama. We, too, are tempted to do the right things in the wrong way, or for the wrong reason. Part of the discipline of Lent is about learning to recognize the flickering impulses, the whispering voices, for what they are, and to have the scripture-fuelled courage to resist. We, too, are part of the ongoing battle for heaven's rule to be established on earth. Every successful fight against temptation is one more step on the road to the ultimate victory.

Today

Lord Jesus, as you saw through the temptations and refused them, give us wisdom to recognize the tempter's voice, and strength to resist.

WEEK 1: SUNDAY

Psalm 32

[1]Happy are those whose transgression is forgiven,
    whose sin is covered.
[2]Happy are those to whom the LORD imputes no iniquity,
    and in whose spirit there is no deceit.
[3]While I kept silence, my body wasted away
    through my groaning all day long.
[4]For day and night your hand was heavy upon me;
    my strength was dried up as by the heat of summer.
[5]Then I acknowledged my sin to you,
    and I did not hide my iniquity;
    I said, 'I will confess my transgressions to the LORD',
    and you forgave the guilt of my sin.
[6]Therefore let all who are faithful offer prayer to you;
    at a time of distress, the rush of mighty waters
    shall not reach them.

⁷You are a hiding-place for me; you preserve me
    from trouble;
    you surround me with glad cries of deliverance.
⁸I will instruct you and teach you the way you should go;
    I will counsel you with my eye upon you.
⁹Do not be like a horse or a mule without understanding,
    whose temper must be curbed with bit and bridle,
    else it will not stay near you.
¹⁰Many are the torments of the wicked,
    but steadfast love surrounds those who trust in the LORD.
¹¹Be glad in the LORD and rejoice, O righteous,
    and shout for joy, all you upright in heart.

A long time ago, when I had just learnt to drive, I ran out of petrol on a lonely country road. I gratefully accepted some fuel from a nearby farmer. What he didn't tell me was that it was a mixture designed not for a car, but for a lawn mower. I got back home all right, but the next day the car behaved like a sick animal, coughing and spluttering. I made it down to the local garage, where the mechanic explained what the wrong fuel does to the engine. There was thick, messy stuff in the carburettor where there should have been clear petrol. He cleaned it out, and I felt – and it was as though the car felt – a huge sigh of relief. Even to hear the engine running smoothly was a delight. Now I was free again, free not to have to worry about the car but to think, more positively, where I might want to go.

That is the mood of this Psalm. It would be wrong to think of it, as some do when the question of sin and confession comes up, as a gloomy poem. Some Christian traditions these days seem to do as little 'confessing' as they can, in case it spoils the happy mood they want to maintain. But that's like trying to carry on driving while the engine is complaining it's running on the wrong stuff. Confession is facing up to what's wrong. The first two verses of the Psalm list four different types of problem: 'offence' or 'transgression' (breaking of a known command), 'sin' (missing the mark of genuine humanness), 'guilt' or 'iniquity' (the murky stuff inside me where there should be clarity and openness) and 'deceit' (the vain attempt to pretend all is well – a very common problem today). And the reason we do this is the same reason I went to the mechanic. As the Psalmist says in verses 3 and 4, it was hard to live like that.

It's only then that we discover why the Psalm declares that people who confess what's wrong inside are 'blessed' or 'happy'. The Psalm is actually a great celebration: it's over! It's gone! It's been dealt with! And instead of the heavy, dark feeling inside, there is a sudden sense of God's presence, protecting and rescuing us (verses 6 and 7).

Only then do we discover that forgiveness isn't just a matter of bringing the bank balance, as it were, back from a huge debt to a balance of zero. Once the car has been cleaned out, we are free to hear a fresh call from God, to hear when he whispers and feel when he nudges, rather than having to be treated like an unbroken horse or mule (verses 8 and 9). A well-trained horse is one that has learnt to sense the rider's hopes and intentions and even to anticipate them. It is as though the mechanic not only fixed the car but showed me on the map some wonderful places to visit that I'd never imagined before.

That's why the poem closes, once again, with celebration. Put off the task of confession and the mess will only get worse, leading to all kinds of trouble. But trust in the Lord – and that trust will often begin by trusting him with our saddest and darkest secrets – and we will find his love surrounding us. It's like going outside on the first spring morning where suddenly you realize it's not cold any more. Lent is a time for discipline, for confession, for honesty, not because God is mean or faultfinding or finger-pointing but because he wants us to know the joy of being cleaned out, ready for all the good things he now has in store.

Today

Father, help me, this Lent, to confess my sin honestly and to celebrate the new life which you give to those who trust you.

WEEK 1: MONDAY

Matthew 5; focused on 5.1–12

[1]When Jesus saw the crowds, he went up the hillside, and sat down. His disciples came to him. [2]He took a deep breath, and began his teaching:

[3]'Wonderful news for the poor in spirit! The kingdom of heaven is yours.

[4]'Wonderful news for the mourners! You're going to be comforted.

[5]'Wonderful news for the meek! You're going to inherit the earth.

[6]'Wonderful news for people who hunger and thirst for God's justice! You're going to be satisfied.

[7]'Wonderful news for the merciful! You'll receive mercy yourselves.

[8]'Wonderful news for the pure in heart! You will see God.

[9]'Wonderful news for the peacemakers! You'll be called God's children.

[10]'Wonderful news for people who are persecuted because of God's way! The kingdom of heaven belongs to you.

[11]'Wonderful news for you, when people slander you and persecute you, and say all kinds of wicked things about you falsely because of me! [12]Celebrate and rejoice: there's a great reward for you in heaven. That's how they persecuted the prophets who went before you.'

The worst mistake we can make about this famous and stunning passage is to see it as a list of rules (you've got to try hard to be poor in spirit, to mourn, to be meek, and so on). It isn't. It's a royal announcement that God is turning the world upside down – or, rather, the right way up.

Come with me into the crowd that has followed Jesus away from the villages and up onto the hillside. What are we hearing? What does it mean to us?

We've been longing for this moment, you see, but we didn't know what it was going to be like. For generations we've all been taught that one day our God, the maker of heaven and earth, would come back to us and set everything right. But as time has gone on it's looked more and more as though he's forgotten us. Arrogant foreign soldiers have pushed their way into our land. Other nations, with their strange and lurid cultures, have taken over some of our towns and changed them into places where decent people wouldn't want to go. And the taxes they make us pay! Anyone would think we were still slaves, instead of God's free people.

But nobody quite knew what it would look like when God came back to us. Some people have said it would be like a great pillar of cloud and fire. Some have said he'd come riding at the head of a great army to defeat the horrible people who are making our lives miserable. Some have even said that we'd better not wait any longer, that perhaps God wants us to act first and then he'll come and help us.

So when we heard about this prophet who was going round the villages healing people and saying that the sovereign rule of heaven was now on the way, we were really excited. What's his plan? What's he saying is going to happen?

And now he's telling us that God is indeed on the move – and that people like us are going to come out on top! We've had our spirits crushed all right; we've been sorrowful, we've been longing for God's way to triumph. It's been a hunger eating away at us inside. And now he's saying that the poor in spirit will inherit heaven's kingdom, that the sorrowful will be comforted, that the hungry will be satisfied. All right! This is what we've been waiting for! But how will it happen? What do we have to do? What are his plans for making it happen?

15

Well, he's saying some other things, too. He's saying that it's the meek who will inherit the earth – not the rich, the powerful, the violent or the pushy. Some people in the crowd don't like that. It sounds like a cop-out to them. And he's saying that the merciful and the peacemakers are the ones who will receive God's mercy, who will be called God's children (we think all the people of Israel are God's children; it sounds as though he's saying that God is reshaping Israel itself!). That's not going to please those who want to fight and kill to make God's will happen.

And then he's saying that it's going to be tough. People are going to hate us and persecute us. Well, we've had plenty of that already, so what's new? It sounds as though he's saying that God is doing a new thing – and that like the ancient prophets many of our own people won't like it. He wants us to follow him, even though it's going to be unpopular.

I don't know where this is leading. But I've never heard anyone speaking like this before. It's a whole new way of being God's people. It's a whole new way of being human. Well, we've tried everything else. Maybe, after all, this is what it's going to look like when God comes back to rescue us. I'm ready to sign up. What about you?

Today

Lord Jesus, help us to hear your voice, to accept your challenge, and to follow you in the way of your kingdom.

WEEK 1: TUESDAY
Matthew 6; focused on 6.5–15

[5]"When you pray, you mustn't be like the play-actors. They love to pray standing in the synagogues and on street corners, so that people will notice them. I'm telling you the truth: they have received their reward in full. [6]No: when you pray, go into

16

your own room, shut the door, and pray to your father who is there in secret. And your father, who sees in secret, will repay you.'

[7]'When you pray, don't pile up a jumbled heap of words! That's what the Gentiles do. They reckon that the more they say, the more likely they are to be heard. [8]So don't be like them. You see, your father knows what you need before you ask him.

[9]'So this is how you should pray:

Our father in heaven,
May your name be honoured
[10]*May your kingdom come*
May your will be done
As in heaven, so on earth.
[11]*Give us today the bread we need now;*
[12]*And forgive us the things we owe,*
As we too have forgiven what was owed to us.
[13]*Don't bring us into the great Trial,*
But rescue us from evil.

[14]'Yes: if you forgive people the wrong they have done, your heavenly father will forgive you as well. [15]But if you don't forgive people, neither will your heavenly father forgive you what you have done wrong.'

At the very heart of Jesus' vision of the kingdom – of heaven's kingdom coming on earth – we have a picture of one person, secretly in their own room, praying.

Prayer is a mystery. I've often heard people saying, with a sneer, 'It doesn't go beyond the ceiling, you know.' But the point of prayer, at least the way Jesus saw it, is that it doesn't have to. Your father, he says, is there in the secret place with you. He sees and knows your deepest thoughts and hopes and fears. He hears the words you say. He hears, too, the things you can't put into words but want to lay before him anyway. Prayer, in fact, isn't a mystery in the sense of 'a puzzle we can't understand'. Prayer is a symptom, a sign, of *the* mystery: the fact that heaven and earth actually mingle together. There are times when they interlock; there are places where they overlap. To pray, in this sense, is to claim a time and place – it can be anywhere, any time – as one of those times, one of those places.

If prayer is about heaven and earth overlapping in time and space, it's also about them coming together in matter, in the stuff of this world, the clay from which we are made. To pray, in this sense, is to claim – think about it and realize just how daring this is! – that the living God, enthroned in heaven, can make his home with you, within you. To make this point vividly, go into your room in secret and pray there. Take God seriously.

But, when you do so, realize one more thing. If prayer is about heaven and earth coming together at one time, in one place, within the lump of clay we call 'me', then it's going to change this person called 'me'. In particular, it's going to make me a forgiver. Jesus was quite clear about this. All of us have been hurt, wounded, slighted, annoyed by other people. How much more have we ourselves done that to God! Yet we want him to be with us, to hear us, and – yes! – to forgive us. How can we not be forgivers too?

So the great prayer comes together. Utterly simple, utterly profound. A child can learn it; an old, wise saint will still be going deeper into it. Heaven is not far away, and it's where we meet the God who, with breathtaking confidence, we can call 'Father'. Familiarity must not imply contempt. His very name is holy, and we must honour it as such. And what we most want – the strange phenomenon of which prayer itself is a supreme example! – is that his kingdom should come and his will be done *on earth as in heaven*. When we pray, we pray *for* that goal but we also pray *within* that promise.

We then place our needs, whether simple or complex, within that framework. Bread for the day ahead. Forgiveness of debt – the debts we owe to God, the debts too (this may surprise some) we owe one another. And then, importantly, rescue: rescue from the time of testing, of trial, whether that be personal temptation, frequently repeated, or the 'tribulation' which Jesus, like many others of his day, believed would come upon the world before God's deliverance finally dawned.

And rescue, too, from the evil one. Much of Jesus' public career was a battle with the powers of darkness. That isn't surprising, since he was announcing that God was taking back control of the world from those powers. When we pray this prayer, we are caught up in that battle, too. But we don't face the danger alone. We claim his victory, his rescue, rather than face danger alone, his deliverance.

The mystery of prayer. This prayer lies at the very centre of the 'sermon on the mount'. It should be at the centre of our life, our own kingdom-obedience.

Today

Lord, teach us to pray; teach us to forgive; make us your people. Yours is the kingdom, the power and the glory.

WEEK 1: WEDNESDAY
Matthew 7; focused on 7.15–23

[15]'Watch out for false prophets. They will come to you dressed like sheep, but inside they are hungry wolves. [16]You'll be able to tell them by the fruit they bear: you don't find grapes growing on thorn-bushes, do you, or figs on thistles? [17]Well, in the same way, good trees produce good fruit, and bad trees produce bad fruit. [18]Actually, good trees *can't* produce bad fruit, nor can bad ones produce good fruit! [19]Every tree that doesn't produce good fruit is cut down and thrown on the fire. [20]So: you must recognize them by their fruits.

[21]"Not everyone who says to me, "Master, master" will enter the kingdom of heaven; only people who do the will of my father in heaven. [22]On that day lots of people will say to me,

"Master, master – we prophesied in your name, didn't we? We cast out demons in your name! We performed lots of powerful deeds in your name!"

[23]"Then I will have to say to them,

"I never knew you! You're a bunch of evildoers – go away from me!"'

One of the great lies of our time is to suppose that because Jesus brings forgiveness, and urges us to be forgiving people, meek and gentle, there is no sharp edge to his message. To hear some people, you'd think the whole of the Christian message was simply a call to accept one another, never to judge another person. Indeed, doesn't Jesus himself tell us not to judge, at the start of this very chapter (7.1)? That verse is quoted again and again by people who would do well to ponder this present passage.

Jesus is quite clear that there are such persons as false prophets, as people who appear to be his followers but who in fact have never known him. Life would be a lot simpler if we could tell at a glance who the true and the false prophets were, but the only guide Jesus offers is the picture of the tree. Sooner or later – and it may be a lot later, or it may happen quite suddenly – the fruit of someone's life will appear, and then you can tell whether they were real or whether they were fooling themselves and others.

In Jesus' own day there was no shortage of such people. Jesus spoke more than once about people who would turn up and declare that they were prophesying in his name, or in God's name, and would lead people astray. The second and third generation of the church faced the same problem, and developed an interesting rule of thumb: if someone arrives claiming to be a prophet, *but asking for money*, they are false.

We might expand that into the usual trio: money is so often linked with sex and power. Some false teachers offer their followers sexual licence in contrast to Jesus' rigorous standard, as in 5.27–30, 15.19–20 and 19.3–12; part of the lie, today, is that Jesus didn't mind about such things. Others are eager for personal power, as you can tell when someone challenges them. And, yes, some today are in it for the money.

When Jesus uses the image of the tree, he is drawing, as so often, on an ancient biblical picture. The first Psalm speaks of God's true people like trees planted by streams of water, which will produce fruit at the right time, while the wicked are like chaff blown around by the wind. Jeremiah develops this picture (17.8), thinking of the tree that sends out its roots to look for the water it needs. Lent is a time when we should be doing that: sending out our roots to look for the water of life. The challenge of these verses isn't simply one of learning to recognize true Christian teaching from false. The challenge is to become, ourselves, trees that bear good fruit, people who not only say 'Lord, Lord' when it suits us, but who apply ourselves to the much harder task of discerning and doing God's will.

Today

Gracious Lord, draw our roots to yourself, the living water, so that we may grow strong and bear good fruit.

WEEK 1: THURSDAY
Matthew 8; focused on 8.23–34

[23]So Jesus got into the boat, and his disciples followed him. [24]All of a sudden a great storm blew up on the sea, so that the boat was being swamped by the waves. Jesus, however, was asleep. [25]They came and woke him up.

'Help, Master, help!' they shouted. 'We're done for!'

[26]'Why are you so scared, you little-faith lot?' he replied.

Then he got up and told the wind and the sea to behave themselves, and there was a great calm. [27]The people there were astonished.

'What sort of man is this,' they said, 'that the winds and the sea do what he says?'

[28]So he went across to the other side, to the region of the Gadarenes. Two demon-possessed men met him, coming out of the tombs. They were very violent and made it impossible for anyone to go along that road.

[29]'What is it with us and you,' they yelled, 'you son of God? Have you come here to torture us ahead of the time?'

[30]Some way off from where they were there was a large herd of pigs feeding.

[31]'If you cast us out,' the demons begged Jesus, 'send us into the herd of pigs!'

[32]'Off you go, then!' said Jesus.

So the demons went out of the men and into the pigs. Then and there the entire herd rushed down the steep slope into the lake, and were drowned in the water.

[33]The herdsmen took to their heels. They went off to the town and told the whole tale, including the bit about the demon-possessed men. [34]So the whole town came out to see Jesus for themselves. When they saw him, they begged him to leave their district.

Let's go on that boat and think what it was like. It's a small lake, as lakes go, but sudden storms come sweeping down from the hills. All of us in the boat know of people who've been drowned there, of whole boats that have been swamped and gone to the bottom, of sad homes back in Capernaum or Magdala where there are widows and small children dependent on relatives because the father and his sons didn't come home from a night's fishing.

So we are right to be afraid, aren't we? You can't deny that! And Jesus, who was doing such great things a minute ago on land, is . . . asleep. How can he do that? Doesn't he care? Should we wake him? Well, why not? If he can't help us, who can?

Then it happens. He wakes up and looks at us, a bit cross but not, it seems, because we've woken him but because of something else. We haven't got enough *faith*, he says. Well, we've sailed this lake often enough and we know that it isn't faith that gets you across, it's hard work with the oars and sails! But then he is saying something again – this time, loud and clear, not to us but to the wind and the sea. He's telling them to shut up! Who does he think he is? This is crazy!

Only it isn't. The wind dies down. The sea becomes very, very still, like a screaming child suddenly pacified. And our question 'Who does he think he is?' turns into a different question: *Who is he?* What sort of man is this?

We've heard the old stories about God telling the wind and the sea to open up a way for his people to pass over. We've heard about Jonah, about Noah. We know the ancient, mysterious story about God making the world in the first place by replacing the waters of chaos with his new creation. We've always wanted this God to come back to rescue us. But we never thought it would be like this. And we never thought we'd have to wake him up to make it happen. But – wait a minute? Isn't that in the old scriptures, too? Didn't the Psalms sometimes shout to God to wake up and sort out the mess?

When we get to the other side, it's someone else doing the shouting. A madman – actually, two of them; and they're yelling at Jesus. Something's got into them. We don't understand it but that's the only explanation. Maybe it's because we're off Jewish territory, this side of the lake. That's why there's a herd of pigs over there; you'd never get that in proper Jewish farms, of course. But now the men are begging Jesus – or rather, it seems to be the strange voices that are coming from the men – to send them into the herd of pigs. There must be evil spirits in there, doing the talking. And Jesus tells them to go. A sudden cold wind, and then it's all stamping and snorting and off they go – over the steep hill and down into the lake. Not surprisingly, the lads in charge of the pigs take to their heels as well. For two pins I'd go too; this is getting too scary for words.

But the heart of it is this. Not only the question we felt on the lake: Who is Jesus? But the question we now can't avoid: Is this what it looks like when God's kingdom begins to arrive on earth as in heaven? Does it mean that some sort of cosmic battle is now in progress, with the storm on the one hand and the evil spirits on the other trying as it were to attack Jesus, to stop him bringing heaven's rule to bear on this dangerous and distracted world of ours? What's that going to mean for us? What's it going to mean for *him*?

Today

Lord of wind and sea, help us to follow you, whatever the questions, wherever you lead.

WEEK 1: FRIDAY

Matthew 9; focused on 9.9–17

[9]As Jesus was walking along, he saw a man called Matthew sitting at the tax-office.

'Follow me!' he said to him. And he rose up and followed him.

[10]When he was at home, sitting down to a meal, there were lots of tax-collectors and sinners there who had come to have dinner with Jesus and his disciples. [11]When the Pharisees saw it, they said to his disciples,

'Why does your teacher eat with tax-collectors and sinners?'

[12]Jesus heard them.

'It isn't the healthy who need a doctor,' he said, 'it's the sick. [13]Go and learn what this saying means: "It's mercy I want, not sacrifice." My job isn't to call upright people, but sinners.'

[14]Then John's disciples came to him with a question.

'How come,' they asked, 'we and the Pharisees fast a good deal, but your disciples don't fast at all?'

24

[15]'Wedding guests can't fast, can they?' replied Jesus, '– as long as the bridegroom is with them. But sooner or later the bridegroom will be taken away from them. They'll fast then all right.'

[16]'No one', he went on, 'sews a patch of unshrunk cloth onto an old coat. The patch will simply pull away from the coat, and you'll have a worse hole than you started with. [17]People don't put new wine into old wineskins, otherwise the skins will split; then the wine will be lost, and the skins will be ruined. They put new wine into new skins, and then both are fine.'

Those of us who now use computers take it for granted that they will have a large internal memory. This is stored on what is called a 'hard disk', as opposed to what we used to have, back in the 1980s, which was a 'floppy disk', which you had to put into the computer and take out again. They didn't hold much information, and you always had to be putting them in and taking them out. It was a nuisance. But you get quite attached to the machines you use a lot, and I remember trying to get a technician to fit a hard drive and disk into the old machine I had been using and wanted to carry on using.

Eventually, as we discussed it, he took a deep breath. 'What you need', he said, 'is not to add more bits onto this old machine. What you need is a new machine.'

That wasn't what I (or my bank manager) wanted to hear. But he was right. The new machine duly arrived, and I quickly realized it was, of course, what I had been needing for some time.

If we get attached to computers and other machines, we get far more attached to the traditional ways in which we have organized and run our lives. And though we all know that things could be better, we all hope that we can simply add the better bit on to the way we do things at the moment, so that we won't have to change too much, if at all.

This is a challenge every generation has to face, but for Jesus and his contemporaries it was massive. They had lived for many centuries with a traditional way of life. They assumed, naturally enough, that if and when their God came back to rescue them he would support and vindicate that way. And Jesus was telling them that something new was happening. God was indeed doing what he'd always said, but the old machines they had been working with – the things they'd expected to happen – simply weren't adequate for this new moment.

They were wanting God to put the world right, with themselves coming out on top as the ones who'd always been on his side. What they hadn't realized was that God would do this for individuals, too, including individuals who up to then had *not* been on his side. Jesus used a picture for this: the doctor doesn't go round visiting people who are fit and well, but people who are sick and poorly. In other words: he wasn't just supporting the status quo. He was doing something much better, much more exciting, much more encouraging for people like us.

In particular, he was replacing an overall mood of sadness and longing with an overall mood of celebration and hope. They used to fast regularly, to remember the times long ago when their nation had suffered awful disasters. Jesus was coming to do something that would always be remembered with celebration – so fasting wasn't appropriate! That was revolutionary. But it was appropriate.

We today fast during Lent, to remind ourselves of the sorrow and sin that still abounds in the world and in our own lives. But we do so as a people whose basic mode of life is celebration. God has brought the new world into being in and through Jesus. Don't try to put the new cloth on the old coat, or the new wine into old bottles. God is making everything new, and he's inviting us to the party.

Today

Thank you, gracious Lord, that you are the doctor who has come to cure us. Help us to celebrate your new life with gratitude and love.

WEEK 1: SATURDAY
Matthew 17.1–9

¹After six days Jesus took Peter, James, and James's brother John, and led them off up a high mountain by themselves. ²There he was transformed in front of them. His face shone like the sun, and his clothes became as white as light. ³Then, astonishingly, Moses and Elijah appeared to them. They were talking with Jesus.

⁴Peter just had to say something. 'Master,' he said to Jesus, 'it's wonderful for us to be here! If you want, I'll make three shelters here – one for you, one for Moses, and one for Elijah!'

⁵While he was still speaking, a bright cloud overshadowed them. Then there came a voice out of the cloud. 'This is my dear son,' said the voice, 'and I'm delighted with him. Pay attention to him.'

⁶When the disciples heard this, they fell on their faces and were scared out of their wits. ⁷Jesus came up and touched them.

'Get up,' he said, 'and don't be afraid.'

⁸When they raised their eyes, they saw nobody except Jesus, all by himself.

⁹As they were coming down the mountain, Jesus gave them strict instructions. 'Don't tell anyone about the vision,' he said, 'until the son of man has been raised from the dead.'

Imagine yourself as a fifth member of the party, going up the mountain with Jesus leading the way, Peter beside him, and James and John following too. The last days and weeks have been utterly bewildering. Nothing like this has happened to you before, or to any of the others. Within a short time, you've got to the point where you really do believe that Jesus is

God's Messiah, his anointed one, the one who will make God's kingdom a reality on earth as in heaven. But how is this going to happen? What will it mean?

It's all so new . . . and one of the things some of your friends are saying, back home, is that Jesus can't really be the one God is sending to rescue Israel and transform the world. He seems so different from what they'd imagined. You know that in yourself. You'd had a vague idea of a warrior king on a white horse, or of a new, strict teacher of the ancient law, insisting on sterner obedience to God's commandments. And Jesus – well, Jesus did indeed make it clear that God's commands mattered deeply, but that was in the context of him healing people, celebrating God's kingdom with all kinds of unlikely people, so that somehow, when he was around, holiness seemed different: exciting, liberating, rather than constricting and gloomy. So it seems to you, along with Peter and the others, that though this isn't what you thought the Messiah would look like he can't really be anybody else.

It's long way up the mountain. Walking, walking, not much being said. Then suddenly a sense of something happening. Your eyes are deceiving you. It's a trick of the light. No, it's a new sort of light – and it's coming from Jesus himself! Jesus is shining, brighter and brighter! And then something else is happening. He's talking to two men, two timeless, ageless figures. You hear enough of what they're saying to know that these are Moses, the great lawgiver, and Elijah, the great prophet. This is overwhelming. Moses, in the old stories, went up the mountain to meet God. So did Elijah. Now we have come up with Jesus and we're meeting Moses and Elijah. All the stories are rushing together. But they're making something quite new, and we're part of it.

Then Peter is speaking. 'This is it! This is wonderful! Let's stay here for ever! We can make booths right here, for you, Jesus, for Moses and for Elijah!' Great idea, you think. This is heaven on earth – heaven and earth coming together at last. This is what we've always longed for. Jesus really is the Messiah. He isn't overthrowing the law and the prophets; he's fulfilling them.

And then it happens. The Voice. People said they heard a voice when Jesus was baptized by John, and now it comes again. 'This is my Son, my Beloved; I am delighted in him. You must listen to him.' Did you imagine it? No, you all heard it, and you all found your legs giving way underneath you with sheer terror. And then it was over. Just Jesus by himself. Don't tell anyone, he says, until the Son of Man has been raised from the dead.

This was all as bewildering and confusing in the first century as it is for us, reading it today. But what it meant at the time, and what it means now, is clear. Jesus was and is God's Messiah, his chosen one, fulfilling the ancient scriptures, bringing the age-old hope into reality. He was and is the ultimate place where heaven and earth meet. And if you stick with Jesus, it'll happen again. Not necessarily people shining like lights – though that has sometimes happened. But people, and places, full of a sense of God's presence and purpose. Usually, when this happens, it's the result of people taking Jesus very seriously. And usually, when it happens, it is in the middle of a time of great testing and trouble. So it was with Moses and Elijah. So it would be with Jesus. So it may well be with us.

Today

Lord Jesus, Son of the living God, show us your glory, and give us ears to listen to what you have to say to us.

WEEK 2: SUNDAY

Psalm 121

¹I lift up my eyes to the hills–
     from where will my help come?

²My help comes from the LORD,
  who made heaven and earth.
³He will not let your foot be moved;
  he who keeps you will not slumber.
⁴He who keeps Israel
  will neither slumber nor sleep.
⁵The LORD is your keeper;
  the LORD is your shade at your right hand.
⁶The sun shall not strike you by day,
  nor the moon by night.
⁷The LORD will keep you from all evil;
  he will keep your life.
⁸The LORD will keep
  your going out and your coming in
  from this time on and for evermore.

I must have sung this Psalm a hundred, perhaps a thousand, times before I stopped to think about the famous first verse. (I have seen it carved above doors and mantelpieces in mountainous parts of the country, sometimes in Latin.) 'I lift my eyes to the hills': it evokes a romantic picture of the Psalmist gazing up into craggy heights with awe and wonder. And the old translation made it seem as though the next line ('from whence comes my help') was a reference to the hills themselves: I look up to the hills, because that's where my help comes from.

But of course the opening lines mean nothing of the sort. In fact, it is as the Psalmist looks to the hills that he realizes that they are *not* the source of his help: his help comes from a much greater place, indeed a person, namely the God who made them (and everything else as well) in the first place. Actually, the Psalmist might even be looking to the hills not as a pleasant and helpful sight, but as a source of danger: Jerusalem, surrounded by hills, could be the victim of a surprise attack. But even if we don't go that far, the opening of the Psalm appears to *contrast* the hills with the Lord himself,

Yahweh, the creator God – even if only to say that if the hills appear great and powerful, the God who made them is far, far more powerful again.

The Psalm then launches out into a sustained praise of God as the one who watches over Israel, moving from the Psalmist's own trust ('my help' in verse 1) to an invitation: Yahweh will do this for you, too. He will not let *your* foot be moved; he keeps *you*; and so on. It's worth turning this back into a claim that we make on our own behalf: Gracious Lord, you made heaven and earth; now, I pray, don't let *my* foot be moved, don't go to sleep while you're watching over *me*, be *my* shade on my right hand, keep *me* from all evil, preserve *my* going out and coming in. Whether we're on the move, resting, working, leaving home and returning – at every point, the Psalm promises that the world's creator will be with us and guard us.

But if we stop there, we've only made our way into the first level of the Psalm. Lent is a great time for pausing and pondering, for reading more deeply and, perhaps, more slowly. This short Psalm is a good place to see some of the other depths. In particular, we might contemplate the fact that Jesus himself made the Psalms his own prayer book, and doubtless knew most if not all of them by heart. What did it mean for him to pray these, up in the hills perhaps, as a boy, as a young man, as the 30-year-old coming to terms with the strong and clear vocation that it was time to act? What did it mean for him to realize that the unsleeping God, who had guarded him all his life, was now asking him to go to the unguarded place, the ultimate danger zone, the hill outside Jerusalem where he would go to his final great work but would not return home in the normal way?

As we think of Jesus fulfilling and transcending this Psalm, our hearts go out as well to all those who live with the times when it seems as though God has indeed been asleep, as though the sun and the moon are hostile, as though all kinds of evil

31

have won the day, and the comforting business of going out and coming in has been cancelled for ever by sickness, accident or a roadside bomb. Somehow, in Jesus, the promises come true again but at a different level. To see this takes courage and perseverance. As we pray this Psalm with God's suffering world on our hearts, let us pray particularly that the gap which to us seems so large, between the help promised here and the dire needs of the world, will be narrowed. And let us pray that we who take comfort in this Psalm may bring that comfort to others who need it.

Today

Almighty God, creator of heaven and earth, in your mercy watch over us and all your people. Give us outward safety and an inward trust in you which will enable us to bring help to others.

WEEK 2: MONDAY

Matthew 10.1–15

[1]Jesus called his twelve disciples to him, and gave them authority over unclean spirits, to cast them out and to heal every disease and every sickness.

[2]These are the names of the twelve apostles. First, Simon, who is called Peter ('the rock'), and Andrew his brother; James the son of Zebedee, and John his brother; [3]Philip and Bartholomew, Thomas and Matthew the tax-collector, James son of Alphaeus, and Thaddaeus; [4]Simon the Cananaean; and Judas Iscariot (who betrayed him).

[5]Jesus sent the Twelve off with these instructions.

'Don't go into Gentile territory,' he said, 'and don't go into a Samaritan town. [6]Go instead to the lost sheep of the house of Israel. [7]As you go, declare publicly that the kingdom of heaven is arriving. [8]Heal the sick, raise the dead, cleanse lepers, cast out demons.

'The message was free when you got it; make sure it's free when you give it. [9]Don't take any gold or silver or copper in your belts; [10]no bag for the road, no second cloak, no sandals, no stick. Workers deserve their pay.

[11]'When you go into a town or village, make careful enquiry for someone who is good and trustworthy, and stay there until you leave. [12]When you go into the house give a solemn greeting. [13]If the house is trustworthy, let your blessing of peace rest upon it, but if not, let it return to you. [14]If anyone won't welcome you or listen to your message, go out of the house or the town and shake the dust off your feet. [15]I'm telling you the truth: it will be more bearable for Sodom and Gomorrah on the day of judgment than for that town.'

Every so often, usually just after a change of government, there is a spate of political autobiographies, as former leaders do their best to cash in on the public's hunger to find out 'the inside story'. One of the most fascinating elements of such books, to me, is the description of the early days, when the young and more or less unknown politician gathers friends around him or her, makes sure that they are loyal, and gives them tasks to do as part of the campaign for leadership, part of the means of gathering support.

There is more to Matthew 10 than that, but not less. Jesus calls twelve of his followers – twelve out of several hundred who had been with him on and off up to this point – and gives them instructions, things to do on his behalf. This requires that they have cut their previous ties: there will be no regular fishing for Peter and Andrew, for James and John, while they are going about these new tasks.

Jesus entrusts them with an urgent mission, specifically to 'the house of Israel'. The Jewish people must hear the call of God's kingdom as soon as possible before, as Jesus had already predicted (8.11), the other nations will be brought in (21.43; 28.19). St Paul, reflecting on all this thirty years later, declared that the Messiah had become 'a servant to the circumcised' (that is, the Jewish people), in order to fulfil the ancient promises God had made to their ancestors, and that then

33

the Gentiles, the non-Jews, would glorify God for his mercy (Romans 15.8–9). Matthew is very conscious of the promises to Israel, and of the fact that Jesus was fulfilling them in order that, through that fulfilment, the whole world might become the sphere of God's saving rule.

The Twelve (representing, of course, the ancient Twelve Tribes: Jesus is deliberately symbolizing the fact that God is renewing his people) are to do pretty much the same things that Jesus had been doing: healing, exorcizing, announcing the good news that God was becoming king at last. You might have thought that this good news would be received as such. But Jesus knew that many would reject it, because it didn't correspond to their expectations. They wanted a different sort of kingdom, one that would support and validate their own national and personal ambitions. Jesus therefore warns the disciples that their mission will be rejected by some, even though others will be enthusiastic.

This is an obvious warning for us as well. All of us like to be liked, and want to be wanted. But not everyone – not even the people we might imagine – will be pleased at the news that God is now running the world in a new way, the way Jesus was showing and teaching. The message of 'peace' (verse 13) is wonderful news for some, but it's unwelcome to those who have decided that the only solution is violence. That message, though, is as urgent today as it was two thousand years ago.

Today

Gracious Lord Jesus, make us instruments of your peace, and of your saving kingdom, wherever we go.

WEEK 2: TUESDAY

Matthew 10.16–42; focused on 10.16–25

[16]'See here,' Jesus continued, 'I'm sending you out like sheep surrounded by wolves. So be as shrewd as snakes, and as innocent as doves.'

[17]'Watch out for danger from people around you. They will hand you over to councils, and have you flogged in their synagogues. [18]You will be dragged before governors and kings because of me, as evidence to them and to the nations. [19]But when they hand you over, don't worry how to speak or what to say. What you have to say will be given to you at that moment. [20]It won't be you speaking, you see; it will be the spirit of your father speaking in you.

[21]'One brother will betray another to death; fathers will betray children, and children will rebel against their parents and have them put to death. [22]You will be hated by everyone because of my name. But the one who holds out to the end will be delivered.

[23]'When they persecute you in one town, run off to the next one. I'm telling you the truth: you won't have gone through all the towns of Israel before the son of man comes.'

[24]'The disciple isn't greater than the teacher; the slave isn't greater than the master. [25]It's quite enough for the disciple to be like the teacher, and the slave to be like the master. If they called the master of the house 'Beelzebul', think what they're going to call his family!'

Let's stand on the edge of the crowd and listen as Jesus gives his twelve disciples these next instructions. Some of the Twelve are looking decidedly uncomfortable, but there's nothing they can do about it. Jesus has called them and they're going to have to get on with it.

These words are uncomfortable. Jesus is telling them it's going to be tough. Not just tough in the sense of hard work with no pay and an uncertain future. Tough in the sense that people are not going to like the message. In particular, in this passage, it's clear that word is going to get back to the officials, whether in the Jewish communities or the wider world. And those officials may well take action.

You might have thought that the news that God was becoming king would be something his ancient people, the Jews, were eager to hear. In a sense, you'd be right. But several of them, particularly those in power like the Sadducees, and those who supported King Herod, didn't really want God to be king, or not just now. They were doing all right out of their own position, thank you very much, and didn't relish the idea of being taken down a peg or two. Especially by a bunch of wandering Galileans with news of a strange would-be king who was doing all sorts of things that no respectable king would ever get up to.

What about non-Jewish rulers? Obviously, news that the God of Israel was becoming king would be a threat to them. There had been revolutionary movements before, shouting 'no king but God' and meaning 'no, we don't want to pay Caesar's taxes!' Jesus can forsee that it's going to be as bad, if not worse, as it was then. Families will be divided. Persecution and even assassination may follow.

So what do you think, hearing all this and seeing the reaction? It may all seem quite unrealistic in today's comfortable western world. But the demands of the kingdom are no less today than they were then. As we find ourselves drawn in from the edge of the crowd, Jesus turns to us. What is he going to say? Are we prepared, in our own day, to follow his way even if people sneer, or threaten, or accuse us?

Jesus knew it was urgent. 'You will not have gone through all the towns of Israel before the Son of Man comes,' he said (verse 23). This is very puzzling. It looks as though Jesus is talking about 'the Son of Man' as someone other than himself. He also seems to be saying that this cataclysmic event ('the coming of the Son of Man') will occur not just in their lifetime but within a year or two at most. What's more, we might assume that Matthew wouldn't have reported Jesus as saying something like this unless he thought it was true. So what is it about?

The answer, as we shall see more fully in due course, is that this is heavily coded political language. Jesus is alluding to the picture we find in Daniel 7, a very popular passage at the time. It was widely read as a revolutionary text, speaking of the 'coming' or vindication of 'one like a Son of Man' – this figure 'coming' not to earth, but to God, to receive power and glory. At the moment, all the bystanders would hear would be a reference to 'the great event God has promised, through which his people will be vindicated'. Jesus would later show them there was more to it again than that. But for the moment they – and we, listening in – need to know that God's purpose is going ahead and that we, caught up to our surprise within it, need to act urgently to play our part in sharing the good news of his kingdom.

Today

Give us courage, good Lord, to follow you and to bear whatever suffering or insults may come as a result.

WEEK 2: WEDNESDAY

Matthew 11; focused on 11.1–19

¹So when Jesus had finished giving instructions to the twelve disciples, he went away from there to teach and preach in their towns.

²Meanwhile, John, who was in prison, heard about these messianic goings-on. He sent word through his own followers.

³'Are you the one who is coming?' he asked. 'Or should we be looking for someone else?'

⁴'Go and tell John', replied Jesus, 'what you've seen and heard. ⁵Blind people are seeing! Lame people are walking! Lepers are being cleansed! Deaf people can hear again! The

dead are being raised to life! And – the poor are hearing the good news! [6]And God bless you if you're not upset by what I'm doing.'

[7]As the messengers were going away, Jesus began to speak to the crowds about John.

'What were you expecting to see,' he asked, 'when you went out into the desert? A reed wobbling in the wind? [8]No? Well, then, what were you expecting to see? Someone dressed in silks and satins? If you want to see people like that you'd have to go to somebody's royal palace. [9]All right, so what *were* you expecting to see? A prophet? Ah, now we're getting there: yes indeed, and much more than a prophet! [10]This is the one the Bible was talking about when it says,

See, I'm sending my messenger ahead of you
And he will clear your path before you.

[11]'I'm telling you the truth: John the Baptist is the greatest mother's son there ever was. But even the least significant person in heaven's kingdom is greater than he is. [12]From the time of John the Baptist until now the kingdom of heaven has been forcing its way in – and the men of force are trying to grab it! [13]All the prophets and the law, you see, make their prophecies up to the time of John. [14]In fact, if you'll believe it, he is Elijah, the one who was to come. [15]If you've got ears, then listen!

[16]'What picture shall I give you for this generation?' asked Jesus. 'It's like a bunch of children sitting in the town square, and singing songs to each other. [17]This is how it goes:

You didn't dance when we played the flute,
You didn't cry when we sang the dirge!

[18]'What do I mean? When John appeared, he didn't have any normal food or drink – and people said "What's got into him, then?" [19]Then along comes the son of man, eating and drinking normally, and people say, "Ooh, look at him – guzzling and boozing, hanging around with tax-collectors and the riff-raff."

But, you know, wisdom is as wisdom does – and wisdom will be vindicated!'

Jesus is here being put on the spot. Today, when interviewers try to force politicians to say things they didn't really want to let out, they tend to prevaricate, to ignore the question, or even to tell downright lies. We have print and electronic media that can take any sentence uttered by a public figure and beam it round the globe in an instant. In Jesus' day they had something almost as powerful, and just as deadly: the rumour mill. Anything you said in one village might precede you to the next. Anything someone like Jesus said about kingship, about God's new purposes coming to pass, might easily land on the desk of the present would-be king of the Jews, Herod Antipas. So, when the awkward question comes, he has truthful but elusive answers ready.

The question was asked by John the Baptist, who was in prison after annoying Herod with his preaching. (John had been saying, among other things, that Herod should not have taken his brother's wife. Accusing someone of blatant immorality was certainly to be taken as a political comment: such a person could hardly be the true king of the Jews. No wonder Herod was annoyed.) But John had pointed to Jesus himself, and had declared that he was God's chosen one, the coming Messiah. Jesus, in other words, was the reality, and Herod just a cheap imitation.

Now Jesus had been healing people, announcing that God was becoming king – but he hadn't marched on Jerusalem, he hadn't launched an attack on Herod, the present wicked usurper. What's more, he hadn't rescued his own poor cousin from Herod's clutches. So: 'Are you the one who is to come, or should we be looking for someone else?' It's the natural question.

But Jesus cannot simply give it the natural answer. To say 'yes' is to send a message directly to Herod via the rumour mill: You, Herod, are supposed to be 'king of the Jews', but now there's someone else going around saying it's him instead. Not the sort of thing a king likes to hear. So Jesus speaks instead in biblical terms. The great prophets, notably Isaiah 35, had predicted a coming time of blessing and healing for God's people. This is coming true in his own work. 'Blessed is the one who takes no offence at me,' he says: in other words, this is what the Messiah is supposed to look like, and if you were expecting something else it's you that needs to adjust your picture!

But then Jesus makes two other points, more cryptic still. First, he asks the crowds why they came out into the wilderness – already knowing the answer, that they came to see John. What were they looking for? A reed shaken in the wind? They would all know that this referred to Herod Antipas, who had a Galilean reed as the emblem on his coins. Or someone clothed in silks and satins? No: you'd had enough of would-be kings, jumped-up little princelings copying the worst habits of Rome and its emperors. This was indeed subversive stuff, but Jesus hasn't said anything that would enable Herod to arrest him too.

But then comes a still more cryptic, powerful saying. The crowds had come to see 'a prophet, and more than a prophet'. Jesus has worked the conversation round. John the Baptist is the greatest man who ever lived; 'yet the least in the kingdom of heaven is greater than he . . . and he is Elijah who is to come.' No wonder he had to say, after that, 'If you've got ears, then listen!' He was speaking in riddles. If John is the greatest man ever, but since then something new has happened which introduces a whole new value-scale, then it can only be that the 'new' thing that has happened is Jesus' own presence, Jesus' own work. If John is Elijah, Jesus is the one whom Elijah was going to announce as imminent . . . which makes him at least Israel's Messiah. Perhaps even the living embodiment of Israel's returning, judging God.

When Jesus says that the kingdom has been breaking in violently, and that violent people are trying to snatch it, what he seems to be saying is that God's kingdom had indeed been decisively launched in his work, and that those bent on violent revolution were trying to get in on the act. That would of course provoke Herod all the more, and indeed – as happens sometimes in our own world – someone who is determinedly pursuing an agenda of violence will not welcome the news of God's kingdom of peace and healing.

The crowds, meanwhile, just don't get it. John looked too crazy, Jesus looks too normal. Sometimes even Jesus just had to plough on, realizing that people hadn't understood, but going ahead anyway. Sometimes we have to do the same.

Today

Lord, give us grace to recognize you, to hail you as our Lord and King, and to follow you even when we too are misunderstood.

WEEK 2: THURSDAY
Matthew 12.1–21; focused on 12.15–21

[15]Jesus discovered the plots against him, and left the district. Large crowds followed him, and he healed them all, [16]giving them strict instructions not to tell people about him. [17]This was so that what was spoken through Isaiah the prophet might come true:

[18]Look! Here's my servant, whom I chose;
My beloved one, my heart's delight.
My spirit I will place on him,
And he'll announce my justice
To the whole wide world.
[19]He will not argue, nor will he
Lift up his voice and shout aloud;
Nobody in the streets will hear

His voice. [20]He will not break the damaged
Reed, or snuff the guttering lamp,
Until his judgment wins the day.
[21]The world will hope upon his name.

To get the full flavour of what's going on here, you should really read not just Matthew 12, but Isaiah 42 as a whole. Actually, even that isn't really enough, because Isaiah 42 is a key passage within a much larger unity, Isaiah 40—55 . . . maybe you should set aside some time later on and read those 16 chapters right through. Imagine yourself in Matthew's congregation. Ask yourself what he's trying to tell you by quoting from that great prophecy.

We have already seen that for Matthew, and for Jesus himself, Jesus' public career was the fulfilment of the ancient prophecies. Not just 'fulfilment' in the sense of a few random long-range predictions that were now at last 'coming true' in an isolated fashion. Rather, 'fulfilment' in the sense of a mountain climber who, after several days of hiking, sheer rock faces, ice floes and so on, is now standing on the summit ridge with the peak of the mountain at last in sight. 'Fulfilment' in the sense of a couple who have endured a long engagement while one was called away on urgent business and who now, at last, can hear the wedding bells ringing as they make their way to the church. Jesus is the 'fulfilment' of scripture in that sense. He brings its long, winding story to the place it was meant to go all along.

When Matthew quotes these verses from Isaiah 42, then, he isn't just suggesting a distant resemblance between Jesus' commands to silence (12.16) and the humble behaviour of Isaiah's 'servant of the Lord'. He is indicating that this 'servant' passage and the others like it, which reach their own climax with the servant's death in chapter 53, are a key part of the build-up of the ancient story. It is all driving forward, looking eagerly ahead, to an ultimate moment in which all the meaning built up over the centuries would be displayed in one extraordinary burst of fulfilment. Every bit of the 'servant' prophecies points to Jesus, Matthew believed. Here, nearly half way through his gospel, he wants to rub our noses in the fact. He could assume that many in his audience would know the whole section of Isaiah quite well. We, who probably don't know it quite so well, may need to catch up.

The point he is making, underneath it all, is that of a different kind of kingdom, an alternative model of kingship. John the Baptist had misunderstood what Jesus was up to, hoping that he might be the sort of leader who would mount a rescue operation and get him out of prison, and he had to be put right. James and John, later on in the story, were eager to have the best seats when Jesus became king, and they too needed to be put right (20.20–28). In the same way, Matthew is keen to point out here that Jesus is redefining what God's kingdom looks like, and hence what being God's Messiah might actually mean.

In fact, of course, what he says here is exactly in line with the Sermon on the Mount. The meek will inherit the earth, and Jesus is leading the way. God's kingdom belongs to the humble, and Jesus is showing how it's done. The kingdom of heaven belongs to those who suffer, are persecuted, and even killed, because they are following God's way . . . and Jesus will go ahead of them in that, too. Matthew, by quoting this passage here, is pointing forwards all the way to the climax of his gospel, when Jesus will be 'enthroned' as 'king of the Jews' by being nailed to the cross.

There is, to be sure, great comfort for us in all of this. If God's kingdom came the same way that earthly kingdoms come, by force of arms and military victory, the weak and the vulnerable would once more come off worst. But God does things the other way up, and we should all be thankful for that. In particular, those of us who struggle from time to time in our faith and discipleship should take heart from

Isaiah's words, applied here to Jesus: he will not break a bruised reed, or quench a smouldering wick. His task, and his delight, is gently to fan into flames what was smouldering, gently to strengthen and firm up the weak, bruised faith, hope and love that we have at the moment. Let that be our prayer this Lent.

Today

Humble Lord Jesus, as you reach out to us in your gentle love, help us to find the way to bring your kingdom in our own day.

WEEK 2: FRIDAY
Matthew 12.22–50; focused on 12.27–32

[27]'What's more, if I cast out demons by Beelzebul, whose power are your people in league with when they cast them out? Yes, they'll tell you what's what! [28]But if I'm casting out demons because I'm in league with God's spirit – well, then, God's kingdom has arrived on your doorstep!

[29]'Look at it like this. Suppose you want to break into a strong man's house and steal his belongings. How are you going to do that unless you first tie up the strong man? Then you can plunder his house to your heart's content. [30]If you're not with me, you're against me. Unless you're gathering the flock with me, you're scattering it.

[31]'So let me tell you this: people will be forgiven for every sin and blasphemy; but blasphemy against the spirit will not be forgiven. [32]If anyone speaks a word against the son of man, it will be forgiven. But if anyone speaks a word against the holy spirit, it won't be forgiven, either in the present age or in the age to come.'

Just in case anyone thought that the vision of a gentle, humble Messiah meant that he would be a pushover for every evil power that came along, the present passage sets the balance straight. One of the things everybody knew about the coming

44

Messiah was that he would fight God's battles and rescue his people. The Bible had said so.

But what is the real battle? For Jesus, it wasn't the battle they all expected him to fight – with the occupying Roman troops, or with Herod and his supporters, or perhaps even with the Sadducees and their would-be aristocratic clique in charge of Jerusalem and the Temple. Jesus' followers probably thought he would fight one or all of them. Having watched as he did many other remarkable things, it was quite easy for them to believe that he could fight a supernatural battle against these natural enemies. Jesus himself spoke, later on, of being able to call several legions of angels to his help.

But on that occasion he refused; because that was the wrong sort of battle to be fighting. In fact, as gradually becomes clear, the real battle is against violence itself, against the normal human wickedness that shows itself in the desire for brute force to win the day. If you fight fire with fire, fire still wins. And Jesus has come to win the victory *over fire itself*, over the rule of the bullies and the power-brokers, in favour of the poor, the meek, the mourners, the pure in heart. It is precisely because Jesus is right in the middle of the real battle that it is vital not to confuse it with other battles.

The real battle, then, is against the real enemy, who is not the flesh-and-blood enemy of foreign soldiers, or even renegade Israelites. (When the Romans crushed the Jewish rebellion in AD 66–70, more Jews were killed by other Jews, in bitter factional fighting, than were killed by the Romans themselves – and they killed quite a lot.) The real enemy is the power of darkness, the insidious, sub-personal force of death, deceit and destruction that goes in scripture by the name of 'the Satan', which means 'the accuser'. It goes by other names, too; a familiar one was 'Beelzebub', which means literally 'Lord of the flies'.

One of the most familiar tactics of this nasty, underhand enemy is to hurl accusations around, which, even though they

WEEK 2: FRIDAY Matthew 12.22–50

may be absurd, can be painful and damaging. Ironically, it is the accusation in verse 24 that shows how seriously the Pharisees were taking Jesus and his powerful deeds of healing. You don't bother saying that someone is in league with the devil if all they are doing is mouthing platitudes. But Jesus' response shows where things had got to from his point of view: 'If it is by the Spirit of God that I cast out demons, then the kingdom of God has come to you' (verse 28). God's sovereign power is at work – through Jesus; and he has won the right to put it into practice because he has first 'tied up the strong man' (verse 29), which presumably refers back to his initial victory over the dark enemy in his own solitary wilderness temptations (4.1–11). As is so often the case, the initial struggle that an individual has with temptation will, if successful, clear the way for fruitful work in the days and years to come. In fact, one might suggest that precisely the reason for the fierce temptation early on in someone's life, or ministry, is because the enemy knows precisely how important that later work will be, and how vital it is – from that hostile viewpoint! – to sabotage it as quickly and thoroughly as possible.

As well as being conscious of having won that earlier victory, Jesus was also fully conscious, ever since his baptism, that he had been endowed with God's own Holy Spirit, to enable him to do what had to be done. When people discounted him personally, that was one thing. They were entitled to their opinion, however mistaken. But someone who looks at the work of God's own Spirit and declares that it is instead the work of the devil is building a high wall around themselves, preventing any light or grace getting in. It isn't that 'the blasphemy against the Holy Spirit' (verse 31) is a peculiarly bad sin which God will punish in a specially harsh way. It is simply that if I deny the existence of the train that is coming in to the station, or declare that it has been sent to deceive me and take me in the wrong direction, I am automatically stopping myself from getting on it. The Spirit was at work through Jesus, to launch God's kingdom; but if someone looked at what was happening and ascribed it to the devil, they could not possibly benefit from it.

A solemn warning, of course, and one that we should heed carefully. It may be that, in our own day, God will do new things which cut against the grain of what the church, or our contemporary world, had led us to expect or hope for.

Today

Gracious Lord, give us the humility to see you at work, and to work alongside you in the power of the Spirit.

WEEK 2: SATURDAY

Matthew 13; focused on 13.31–33, 44–46

[31]He put another parable to them.

'The kingdom of heaven', he said, 'is like a grain of mustard seed, which someone took and sowed in a field. [32]It's the smallest of all the seeds, but when it grows it turns into the biggest of the shrubs. It becomes a tree, and the birds in the sky can then come and nest in its branches.'

[33]He told them another parable.

'The kingdom of heaven is like leaven,' he said, 'which a woman took and hid inside three measures of flour, until the whole thing was leavened . . .

[44]'The kingdom of heaven', Jesus continued, 'is like treasure hidden in a field. Someone found it and hid it, and in great delight went off and sold everything he possessed, and bought that field.

[45]'Again, the kingdom of heaven is like a trader who was looking for fine pearls, [46]and who found one that was spectacularly valuable. He went off and sold everything he possessed, and bought it.'

'An earthly story with a heavenly meaning.' I used to think that that old Sunday-school definition of a parable was a

harmless comment. I now think it's more likely to be dangerous nonsense. Jesus didn't tell parables to provide friendly
little illustrations of abstract theology. He told parables because what he was doing was so different, so explosive, and
so dangerous, that the only way he could talk about it was to
use stories. These are earthly, and sometimes heavenly, stories
with an emphatically earthly meaning. They explain the full
meaning not of distant timeless truths, but of what Jesus was
up to then and there. *This is what is going on*, they say, *if only
you had eyes to see*. Or, indeed, as Jesus frequently says, ears to
hear.

Jesus' parables invite the hearer to look at the world, and
particularly to look at Jesus himself, in a whole new way. You
can see the force of this if you imagine for a moment the
standard objection to Jesus' announcement of God's kingdom, from that day to this. 'Of course God's kingdom hasn't
come,' say the objectors (including many devout Jews, to this
day). 'Read the newspapers! Look out of the window! If
God's kingdom had really come, the world wouldn't still be in
such a mess!'

And of course they are right – at one level. If 'God's kingdom
coming on earth as in heaven' means the complete abolition
of all evil, and ultimately of death itself, then of course it is not
yet here. But – as Jesus insisted in the passage we looked at
yesterday – if Jesus was indeed winning the victory over the
oldest and deadliest enemy, liberating people who had been
completely taken over by the forces and powers of darkness,
and if he was doing so in the power of God's spirit, then God's
sovereign, saving, healing power was indeed being let loose into
the world in a new, unprecedented fashion. And the sharpest
way of describing that was to say, 'then God's kingdom has
come upon you'.

But another way of saying the same thing, more obliquely
perhaps but ultimately more effectively, was to tell stories. Jesus
told a great many, and lots of them were different ways of

coming at the same point: that yes, the full victory, the final abolition of evil, still remained in the future, but no, that didn't mean that nothing was really happening, that God's kingdom wasn't really present in some way or other.

The stories that make this point most effectively include the two little parables in verses 31, 32 and 33. A grain of mustard seed is tiny. But when it grows, it turns into a large shrub, and the birds can nest in it. What is Jesus saying? 'Don't despise the small beginnings of the kingdom. What I (Jesus) am doing is planting seeds. They may not look much at the moment. But they're going to grow. And when they do, then you'll be surprised at the birds that come to roost.' Many people have detected here a reference to foreign nations coming to share in Israel's privileges.

The same point emerges from the parable of the yeast. I once had a breadmaking machine, and I never tired of the apparent miracle by which a tiny amount of yeast made the whole loaf rise. In the same way, the kingdom-work that Jesus is doing may be small and insignificant. In his whole life he can't have travelled more than a few hundred miles. He met a comparatively small number of people – though considerably more than an ordinary Galilean villager might expect to meet – and, so far as we know, never went and preached before kings or rulers. He wrote no book; television hadn't been invented, so he was never invited to appear on chat shows or *I'm a Celebrity*. And yet the yeast that he stirred into the loaf – the kingdom-work he did in a very short time in a very small place – has leavened the loaf of the whole world. Almost everybody now dates world history in relation to his birth. Even those who do their best to ignore his message still have to refer to him sooner or later. His way of love, forgiveness, humility and service has woven itself into the fabric of many societies, so that even where it's ignored people know that something happened in his life and death that changed the world.

There is more. The yeast hasn't completed its work. The plant that has grown from the mustard seed has further still to go. That's why today's other pair of little parables still matter. The other main message of this chapter is that Jesus is looking for people to sign on, people who are prepared to take his kingdom-movement forward in their own day. Here the stories are about someone finding something of enormous value and selling everything they possess in order to buy it. This could be heard in a rather selfish fashion: if I give up everything else for Jesus I will have a wonderful spiritual life. That is no doubt true, but the kingdom of heaven is far, far more than 'me and my spiritual life' now and salvation in the end. The kingdom of heaven is about God's rule sweeping through the sad, decaying world we live in. That is a goal worth working for! That is a vocation to beat all others. Give up your other treasures, Jesus is saying, and buy this one. Give up the small collection of pearls which have meant so much to you. Here is the biggest, finest one you could ever imagine.

Jesus still holds out that clear, almost teasing invitation to us today. His kingdom is still growing, still meeting sharp opposition to be sure, but still making its way in the world. To be part of that work is the greatest privilege you could imagine.

Today

Lord Jesus, tell us again the story of your kingdom, and draw us to follow you, to find the treasure, to help in the work of making that kingdom grow.

WEEK 3: SUNDAY

Psalm 95

¹O come, let us sing to the LORD;
    let us make a joyful noise to the rock of our salvation!
²Let us come into his presence with thanksgiving;

let us make a joyful noise to him with songs of praise!
³For the LORD is a great God,
    and a great King above all gods.
⁴In his hand are the depths of the earth;
    the heights of the mountains are his also.
⁵The sea is his, for he made it,
    and the dry land, which his hands have formed.
⁶O come, let us worship and bow down,
    let us kneel before the LORD, our Maker!
⁷For he is our God,
    and we are the people of his pasture,
    and the sheep of his hand.
O that today you would listen to his voice!
⁸   Do not harden your hearts, as at Meribah,
    as on the day at Massah in the wilderness,
⁹when your ancestors tested me,
    and put me to the proof, though they had seen my work.
¹⁰For forty years I loathed that generation
    and said, 'They are a people whose hearts go astray,
    and they do not regard my ways.'
¹¹Therefore in my anger I swore,
    'They shall not enter my rest.'

A small boy I knew asked his grandfather, a retired priest, what 'worship' meant. The old man paused. He was over 80 years of age, he said; he had been a clergyman most of his life; and he still found it hard to say exactly what 'worship' meant. Like someone who takes ten thousand breaths every day but still couldn't explain to a medical student what breathing is or why it's important, the old man had worshipped all his life, and led others to do so, but found it more and more mysterious.

This Psalm is one that the old clergyman would have said day by day throughout his life, because in the prayer book he used it was prescribed for every day except Easter. I myself grew up in a church where we sang this Psalm almost every Sunday. And I believe we can learn a great deal about what worship is from seeing what's going on here.

The Psalm is not addressing God directly, but calling on other people to join the poet in doing so, in praising the God he here describes. When you really discover who God is, then it is natural to 'make a joyful noise' (verse 1), to come into God's presence with thanksgiving and make music (that most mysterious of all the arts, itself joining heaven and earth) to acclaim him and proclaim his greatness.

Worship, then, is about contemplating who God is and what he's done, standing in awe and expressing that awe in thanks and praise. In the Jewish and Christian traditions, this always begins with praise to God as creator. Every step of scientific advance should increase this chorus of praise (instead of what happens at the moment, that every new scientific discovery leads someone to claim that this has disproved God's existence!). God isn't part of the natural order, though his presence permeates it. Rather, he is other than and outside it, as different from it, and hence from us, as we are from microbes and atoms – only far more so, since they and we are, at one level, all part of the same stuff. God's power holds together the deepest and the highest places on earth, the unfathomable vastness of the sea and the wonderfully sculpted dry land in all its variety.

That would by itself be enough to call us to worship: perhaps, today, you might spend some time contemplating the astonishing range of God's creation. Out of a small window where I am sitting, I can see several different colours, several types of tree and plant, various different animals, and, not least, the sky itself, a source of endless wonder. A short walk, even in an apparently dull area, can lead to wonder and praise. And if you go out on the sea, or into the mountains, or pause in a richly stocked garden, there is no end of extraordinary and beautiful things for which to give thanks.

As always in scripture, contemplating God as creator leads to the astonishing claim that he is 'our God' (verse 7). God has chosen Israel as his people; and we who believe in Jesus believe him to be the fulfilment of this promise, so that all who belong to Jesus can make the same claim. 'We are the people of his pasture, and the sheep of his hand.' City-dwellers often suppose that animals are basically stupid. Not so. Near where I live, the elderly cows in the field know precisely which noises will signal the arrival of fresh food. They recognize voices and react accordingly. In the Middle East, to this day, the relationship of sheep and shepherd is warm and intimate, a mutual bond of knowing. That's how it should be with God and his people. Here, in the middle of Lent, we should celebrate that and be encouraged.

That's important, because as the final verses of the Psalm remind us (sadly, some churches tend to miss them out), we can't take God for granted. The Israelites, whom God had rescued from Egypt, spent 40 years grumbling and questioning. We are warned against going the same way. The best antidote is to return to worship and praise. An older generation used to sing, 'Count your blessings, name them one by one; and it will surprise you what the Lord has done.' If you include the whole of creation, in its vast scope and tiny detail, among those blessings – as the Psalm encourages you to do – it will not only surprise you. It will take quite a long time.

Today

Sovereign God, we praise you for your wonderful world, and we pray that you will replace our grumbles with gratitude, and our questioning with adoration.

WEEK 3: MONDAY
Matthew 14; focused on 14.22–33

²²Jesus at once made the disciples get into the boat and go on ahead of him to the opposite shore, while he dismissed the

crowds. [23]After he had sent the crowds away, Jesus went up the mountain by himself to pray. When evening came he was there by himself. [24]The boat had already gone some distance from the shore and was being smashed around by the waves, since the wind was against it.

[25]At the very dead of night he came towards them, walking on the water. [26]The disciples saw him walking on the sea and panicked, thinking it was a ghost. They screamed with terror. [27]But Jesus at once spoke to them.

'Cheer up,' he said, 'it's me! Don't be frightened!'

[28]'If it's really you, Master,' said Peter in reply, 'give me the word to come to you on the water.'

[29]'Come along, then,' said Jesus.

Peter got out of the boat and walked on the water and came towards Jesus. [30]But when he saw the strong wind he was afraid, and began to sink.

'Master,' he yelled, 'rescue me!'

[31]Jesus at once reached out his hand and caught him.

'A fine lot of faith you've got!' he said. 'Why did you doubt?'

[32]They got into the boat, and the wind died down. [33]The people in the boat worshipped him.

'You really are God's son!' they said.

Forty years ago I sat in my college room with a friend and we read this passage together. He had come to a living faith in Jesus just a week before. He was still wide-eyed with delight at the sense of Jesus' personal presence within him, and at the changes he could feel happening in his heart and head. But he was also anxious. Is this just a fad? Can I keep it up? Will this just be one of those things that is very exciting for a few weeks, and then will fade, leaving me a bit sad and cynical?

This passage might have been written for someone in that frame of mind. Peter is one of the few characters in the gospels, other than Jesus himself, whom we really get to know. This story is typical of the man we see all through – loyal, impetuous, wanting to do the right thing, then getting it embarrassingly wrong and having to be rescued once more. Many of us can identify with him only too easily.

But before we even get to Peter's bit, notice what has happened. Jesus has just fed five thousand people with what started out as next to nothing. As we know from the other gospels, the crowds were, not unnaturally, very excited at this. Jesus as always was anxious that things shouldn't get out of hand (John tells us that the crowd wanted to seize him and hail him as king then and there, which would have been disastrous). So he quickly sent the disciples away and disappeared up the mountain.

Then it happened. Some time after midnight, as they were still tugging at the oars and getting nowhere, he came to them. Walking on the water.

This is such a strange story that many have sneered at it, but Matthew and the other writers knew perfectly well how strange it was and told it anyway. We have been learning, bit by bit, to see that Jesus seems to have possessed a kind of sovereignty over creation itself. Though our minds boggle at the thought of what that might mean, the story fits this pattern. The disciples, not unnaturally, are scared out of their minds: it must be a ghost! But no; Jesus tells them it's all right. They are not to be afraid. ('Don't be afraid,' by the way, is the most frequently repeated command in the whole Bible – something we all need to remind ourselves in our worrying and frantic world.)

Then it's Peter's turn. Triumph, disaster and rescue. Peter the fisherman knows perfectly well you can't walk on water. But, as we saw in chapter 10, Jesus gave the Twelve power to do the things he'd been doing . . . so maybe with this as well? And, amazingly, it happens. Peter walks towards Jesus. That is the walk of faith which we all take when we hear Jesus' voice and begin to follow him. We know perfectly well the world isn't like this; that money, sex and power are what matters;

that we can't possibly give up our bad habits or keep up a life of prayer and holiness . . . but perhaps we just might, if Jesus himself called us to do it? Yes, he says, I am calling you; and off we set.

But then it all goes wrong. The wind had been there all along, but now Peter noticed it as if for the first time: what am I doing? I must be mad! I can't possibly . . . and he starts to sink. That's how it is for us, too. But the crucial moment is the next one. 'Lord, rescue me!' The simplest of prayers, and one which Jesus loves to answer. That's what he's come for, he said on another occasion, to look for people in need and rescue them. He may then smilingly remind us that we shouldn't have doubted. That's the lesson we need to learn, and it will take time. But he comes into the boat with us; the wind stops; and the result, of course, is worship. I doubt if the disciples quite knew what they meant by 'Son of God' at this point. But there wasn't much else they could say.

I lost touch with my friend after we left college. But just the other day I met someone who attends the same church. He is still going on, trusting Jesus, walking with him, helping others in their own faith. No doubt there have been times when, like Peter, like you and me, he's been tempted to doubt, and has started to sink. But Jesus loves rescuing people. That's what he's come to do.

Today

Lord, give us the faith we need to attempt the impossible for you; and rescue us when our faith suddenly gives out.

WEEK 3: TUESDAY

Matthew 15.1–20; focused on 15.1–9

[1]At that time some Pharisees and scribes came from Jerusalem to Jesus. They had a question for him.

²'Why', they said, 'do your disciples go against the tradition of the elders? They don't wash their hands when they eat their food!'

³'Why', Jesus replied, 'do *you* go against the command of God because of your tradition? ⁴What God said was "Honour your father and mother" and "If anyone speaks evil of father or mother, they must certainly die." ⁵But you say, "If anyone says to father or mother, 'What you might have gained from me is given to God', ⁶they need do no further honour to their father." As a result, you make God's word null and void through your tradition.

⁷'You play-actors! Isaiah had the right words for you in his prophecy:

⁸This people gives me honour with their lips,
Their heart, however, holds me at arm's length.
⁹The worship which they offer me is vain,
Because they teach, as law, mere human precepts.'

'Germs and Jesus!' shouted the seven-year-old son of a friend of mine. 'Germs and Jesus! You keep telling me they're important and I can't see either of them!'

A fascinating response to a pressing parental problem. We tell our children about Jesus. We also, at a different level, explain to them that they must wash their hands because there are things called 'germs' which we can't see but which do nasty things if we don't wash them off.

Jews in the ancient world didn't know what we know about germs (they didn't know what we know about Jesus, if it comes to that) but they knew how important it was to wash before meals. Physical purity, with its echoes of national purity (always important for a small and embattled nation), had been elevated to an art form, with careful rules precisely formulated and exactly observed, at least by those who chose to do so. There was a considerable spectrum in Judaism at the time of Jesus, from those who were eager to find and follow the ancient legal traditions more precisely to those who didn't bother too much, either because they weren't pious or, perhaps, because they weren't well off and couldn't afford the time for all the extra fuss.

The Pharisees were a popular pressure group devoted to keeping one another up to the mark of the strict rules, and doing their best, as far as they could, to apply them to other Jews as well. Physical purity made as much sense then as it does now, and without modern soap and other aids to cleanliness there was a lot of practical wisdom, as well as traditional religion, about the rules. But, as often happens in such systems, rules led to more rules, regulations to more regulations, and the original purpose was always in danger of being lost underneath.

So when the Pharisees challenged Jesus about the fact that his disciples weren't keeping the purity traditions in the proper way, Jesus reacted with a counter-charge of his own. What happens when traditions, however venerable, cut across what scripture itself said? He gave as his example a piece of special pleading. You could, in his day, make a formal declaration that the money that could have been used to support your parents was instead 'given to God' – thus neatly getting out of the open-ended, and often sad and messy, business of looking after the elderly. Scripture has been overthrown, as Isaiah said would happen, by human tradition.

This passage has been seized upon down the years by people eager to make a similar point in relation to the growth of various kinds of tradition within the church. And it has to be admitted that all segments of the church (including, paradoxically, the streams of Protestantism that have protested about other people's 'traditions') are quite capable of producing traditions which manage to get around what scripture actually says. Tradition matters because, so we believe, God hasn't stopped working in the lives of his people by his Spirit. We have learned a lot over the last two thousand years which shouldn't just be thrown away. But there is always the chance, in every branch of the church, that the traditions will take on a life of their own and distort or deny some key bit of scripture. This passage should remind us of that danger. Lent is a good time for the church to examine itself on this question.

Jesus then took the occasion to develop his own vision of purity. He didn't say physical cleanness didn't matter. What he did say was that inner purity was far more important. Following deep strains of thought in scripture itself, he warned that the human heart is the source of the greatest pollution, and that nothing in human tradition can purify it. The implication is clear: Jesus is offering a cure for the polluted heart.

That was the real bone of contention between Jesus and the Pharisees. They were supporting a system which, at its best, was pointing forward to God's great desire to find a purified people for himself. Jesus was claiming that God was now doing this, through him. They were setting up signposts; he claimed to offer the reality which made the signposts redundant. Here is the lesson for us: following Jesus, allowing him to cleanse us through and through, puts us in direct continuity with the ancient scriptures, and enables us to discern the good and the less good in human traditions.

Today

Gracious Lord, teach us so to love you that we may find ourselves transformed by your holiness; and save us from human traditions that would imprison us in our own inventions.

WEEK 3: WEDNESDAY
Matthew 15.21–38; focused on 15.21–28

[21]Jesus left that place and went off to the district of Tyre and Sidon. [22]A Canaanite woman from those parts came out and shouted, 'Have pity on me, son of David! My daughter is

demon-possessed! She's in a bad way!' [23]Jesus, however, said nothing at all to her.

His disciples came up.

'Please send her away!' they asked. 'She's shouting after us.'

[24]'I was only sent', replied Jesus, 'to the lost sheep of the house of Israel.'

[25]The woman, however, came and threw herself down at his feet.

'Master,' she said, 'please help me!'

[26]'It isn't right', replied Jesus, 'to take the children's bread and throw it to the dogs.'

[27]'I know, Master. But even the dogs eat the scraps that fall from their master's table.'

[28]'You've got great faith, haven't you, my friend! All right; let it be as you wish.'

And her daughter was healed from that moment.

Let's listen in on this conversation. Stand in the crowd and see what you think.

We're up north now, away from Galilee. Jesus has already spoken of this region ('the district of Tyre and Sidon') in such a way as to make it clear that he and his Jewish hearers thought of it as non-Jewish, beyond the pale (11.21). Now he's come here, we're not sure why; perhaps to escape, for a while, the controversy hanging in the air after his previous exchange with the Pharisees (15.1–20).

As we watch from the sidelines, suddenly a local woman comes out of the crowd and starts shouting at Jesus. 'Take pity on me, son of David!' Her daughter, it seems, is in a terrible state, tormented by evil spirits. 'Take pity on me, son of David!'

A whisper goes through the crowd. 'Son of David?' That's serious talk. The Jews, down south, may be looking for a coming king, but what would that have to do with us non-Jews? Clearly the woman is desperate. Mothers in the crowd know exactly how she feels. They'd do anything to get help if it was their daughter. Still the woman goes on, 'Take pity on me, son of David!'

We watch to see what's going to happen, but Jesus and his friends are moving on and he's not saying anything. Finally his friends have had enough. 'Tell her to go away! She's shouting after us!' This is a puzzle. We in the crowd thought Jesus was a healer. Why doesn't he heal the little girl? And why don't his followers want him to?

Then, at last, Jesus speaks, and what he says sends a chill through the crowd. 'I was sent only to the lost sheep of the house of Israel.' 'Well,' mutters someone close by, 'so what are you doing here, then? Why come to us if you don't want to help us too?'

We, remembering the previous conversation, may have an answer to that; it was wise to lie low for a bit. And, having followed Jesus for some time now, we realize that what he just said fits with what he had said to the Twelve in 10.5–6: don't go to the Gentiles, only to Israel. Jesus was strongly aware of a commission, a solemn charge he'd received from his Father. His job was to announce God's rule *to his own people, the Jews*. If he began to preach and teach more widely, the Jews would write him off as a traitor. They would never then discover that he had come to fulfil their deepest hopes.

But then the woman comes right up to Jesus and kneels down before him. We hold our breath as the crowd quietens down to listen. 'Lord, help me!'

Then a gasp of horror at Jesus' response. 'It isn't right to take the children's bread and throw it to the dogs.' Dogs! That's what some Jews called non-Jews. Surely Jesus doesn't think in those terms? It's as though he's struggling within himself; he knows what his commission had been and doesn't want to be disloyal, disobedient. What he has to give, he must give to God's ancient people; they must never be able to say that their own coming king ignored them and went elsewhere. And yet . . . he had already said that many would come from east and west and sit down with Abraham, Isaac and Jacob. Could it be that this future promise was already starting to come true, even before he'd finished his mission to Israel?

Normally, when we listen in to conversations Jesus is having, it's other people who set the thing up with comments or questions and Jesus who gives the brilliant punchline. This time it's the other way round. The woman accepts Jesus' point of-view and turns it to her own advantage. 'Yes,' she says, 'but the dogs under the table eat what the children drop!'

We feel the buzz in the crowd. Great line! Well said! Nice job! And Jesus seems to agree. 'You have great faith! As you wish, so let it be done.' And the girl is healed.

And we are left thinking: is *that* what we mean by faith? Faith to see how God's strange plan works, even though it isn't exactly flattering for us? Faith to cling on to everything Jesus says even when it's unexpected, and to pray in those terms rather than assume he's going to do what we want in the way we want it?

Jesus makes to leave. His eyes swing slowly round the crowd, and they pause for a moment on you. 'What is it *you* want from me, then?' he seems to be saying. 'Have you got enough faith to see God's strange plan working its way out and find what you need within it?'

Today

Sovereign Lord, give us the faith to ask for your help, and the humility to receive it on your terms.

WEEK 3: THURSDAY
Matthew 16; focused on 16.21–28

[21]From then on Jesus began to explain to his disciples that he would have to go to Jerusalem, and suffer many things from

the elders, chief priests and scribes, and be killed, and be raised on the third day.

[22]Peter took him and began to tell him off. 'That's the last thing God would want, Master!' he said. 'That's never, ever going to happen to you!'

[23]Jesus turned on Peter. 'Get behind me, satan!' he said. 'You're trying to trip me up! You're not looking at things like God does! You're looking at things like a mere mortal!'

[24]Then Jesus said to his disciples,

'If anyone wants to come after me, they must give themselves up, and pick up their cross, and follow me. [25]Yes: if someone wants to save their life, they must lose it; and if anyone loses their life for my sake they will find it. [26]What use will it be, otherwise, if you win the whole world but forfeit your true life? What will you give to get your life back? [27]You see, the son of man is going to "come in the glory of his father with his angels", and then "he will reward everyone for the work they have done". [28]I'm telling you the truth: some of those standing here will not taste death until they see "the son of man coming in his kingdom".'

The unique city of Venice is now mainly a tourist destination. People come from all over the world to be amazed at its canals, its tiny side-streets, and the wonderful churches, mansions and art galleries. But in the days before air travel Venice was much, much more. It was where the trade routes met, a city which looked east and west, north and south. There you could see Europe and Asia coming by and doing business. Many different strands of culture met and mingled on those canals, in those streets and churches. Venice was one of the most powerful and wealthy cities in the world.

This passage in Matthew is a bit like that. We may come to it in search of a quick lesson, a theme to ponder, a direction for today's prayers. But this is one of the places where the trade routes of Matthew's gospel meet, looking all the way back to Jesus' birth and baptism and all the way on to his death and resurrection. This is where the story of the disciples, who had followed Jesus and believed that he was indeed the Messiah, washes up against the story of Jesus' deeper vocation, that he had to achieve his mission by going to the cross. This is one of the most powerful passages in the gospel. Get this straight, and you'll see how much of the rest works out.

Begin at the end – and let's be clear, from the outset, how much Jesus' words here have been misunderstood. 'There are some standing here who won't taste death before they see the Son of Man coming in his kingdom.' Many have imagined that Jesus meant by this that the whole space–time universe would disappear and leave him and his followers in a new heavenly existence. Since that didn't happen – certainly within a generation! – they have concluded that Jesus was mistaken. That point of view has been extremely common.

But it completely misunderstands what the whole gospel story is about. From start to finish, Matthew's story is about *the strange way in which Jesus became king*. The first two chapters make it clear that he is the king from the line of David, at whose birth Gentile sages come to worship. The closing scene of the gospel makes it clear that with his resurrection and ascension Jesus *has* now 'come in his kingdom': 'all authority in heaven and on earth', he says, 'has been given to me.' Our problem in the modern world has been that we have taken it for granted that Jesus is not, in any sense, currently 'king of the world'. (It certainly doesn't look like it, we tell ourselves.) So we have assumed that he must have been talking about something else. Something that didn't happen.

But the whole point of this story is that Jesus – to the horror of his close friends – was now beginning to tell them that the way he had to become king was *through* suffering and death. They had just declared that they believed he was God's Messiah (verse 16). Peter had been congratulated on recognizing this despite the fact that Jesus wasn't doing lots of things a Messiah might have been supposed to do (raising an army to defeat the Romans, for instance). But now he was saying something as shocking to them as his words to the Canaanite woman in chapter 15 were shocking to the foreign crowds. *The way to the Messianic kingdom is through suffering and death.* Why this is so he doesn't yet explain. That it is so he makes quite clear. And if Peter can't see that, then he is being a 'Satan', an accuser, thinking in mere human categories rather than in God's categories.

The challenge to the disciples, then, turns into the challenge to all of us. Following Jesus means losing your life in order to find it. We squirm and struggle against this, like a fish on a hook. Anything rather than this. But it's the only way. Following Jesus means denying yourself, saying 'no' to the things that you imagine make up your 'self', and finding to your astonishment that the 'self' you get back is more glorious, more joyful than you could have imagined. That's how the kingdom arrived through Jesus' achievement. That's how it spreads today. All the trade routes of Christian theology and discipleship pass through this point.

Today

Teach us, gracious Lord, to follow you all the way where you lead, whatever it costs.

WEEK 3: FRIDAY

Matthew 17; focused on 17.14–20

[14]When they came near the crowd, a man approached and knelt in front of him.

[15]'Master,' he said, 'take pity on my son! He suffers from awful fits which are frightful for him. He often falls into the fire, and often into the water. [16]I brought him to your disciples, but they couldn't cure him.'

[17]'You unbelieving and twisted generation!' responded Jesus. 'How much longer must I be with you? How much longer must I put up with you? Bring him here to me.'

[18]Then Jesus rebuked the demon and it came out of him. The boy was cured from that moment.

[19]The disciples came to Jesus in private. 'Why couldn't we cast it out?' they asked.

[20]'Because of your lack of faith,' Jesus replied. 'I'm telling you the truth: if you have faith like a grain of mustard seed, you will say to this mountain, "Move from here to there", and it will move. Nothing will be impossible for you.

Once more we come close to Jesus in the crowd; and this time let's bring with us someone we know, perhaps someone very close to us, who is in serious need of Jesus' help. Take a moment and think who you want to bring.

Let's recall what has just happened. The disciples have told Jesus he is the Messiah, the one to fulfil Israel's hopes and dreams. He has told them, to their horror, that the way that fulfilment will come is through his own suffering and death. Then, amazingly, he has taken three of them up a mountain and has been transfigured before them, shining like the sun. They have heard God's voice declaring that Jesus is indeed his son, his beloved one.

Meanwhile the other disciples, left behind at the foot of the mountain, have faced a challenge they couldn't deal with. That's perhaps where we are ourselves right now, either with sickness in the family or with an impossible situation at work, or something more sad and secret that it's hard even to mention. So we stand there with them as Jesus shakes his head. Surely his followers have learned the lesson by now? Surely they know that God's power is able to do whatever is needed? Actually, it isn't that easy. They've seen Jesus at work; they have known his power in their lives; but when Jesus goes away for a short while they revert, as we all do, to 'normal' mode. Wonderful things don't happen. Life is tough, and there's nothing that can be done.

But they are wrong. Jesus heals the boy. It's not even clear (to us, and perhaps to them) what the problem was. Epilepsy and demon-possession are two very different things, and it's likely that the loose terminology people used at the time wasn't meant to be medically precise. Anyway, Jesus deals with it. We pause there and hold before Jesus the person we've brought, about whom we seem able to do nothing. We watch as Jesus heals the boy, and we pray for healing for whoever it is on our hearts.

And then he deals with the disciples. You couldn't do it, he says, because of your little faith. He's said it four times already (6.30; 8.26; 14.31; 16.8) and they still don't get it. All it takes in fact, he says, is faith like a grain of mustard seed – an image he's already used for the kingdom itself (13.31). Faith is like a small window through which you can see a vast landscape, and the landscape in question is the sovereign power of the creator God and the overwhelming glory of Jesus himself. We stand at that window, doing our best to wipe it clean from the condensation of our own unbelieving breath, and holding on, as we do so, to those for whom we want to pray.

Jesus spoke of moving mountains – a regular type of exaggeration, no doubt, though they may have heard echoes of the challenge which awaited them on the holy mountain, Jerusalem itself. But sometimes it seems easier to move a mountain, shovelling it with spoons, than to shift the sorrow or sickness from a human heart and life. When you read the stories of remarkable Christians down the years, and in our own time too, again and again you find tales of people who have stood at that window, gazing out on the landscape of God's power and love, and gradually bringing the rest of the world, and the people for whom they were praying, into healing focus in relation to it. We need more people like that. The most important Christians are not the ones who preach great sermons and write great books, but the ones who pray, and pray, and pray some more, sharing the quiet but effective victory of Jesus over all that defaces God's creation.

Today

(Fill in the blank in the prayer with whoever you want to pray for:)

Lord Jesus, you have the power to heal and rescue. Today I pray for ____ who need you so badly. Bring them your healing love, and transform their lives with your grace.

WEEK 3: SATURDAY
Matthew 18; focused on 18.21–35

[21]Then Peter came to Jesus.

'Master,' he said, 'how many times must I forgive my brother when he sins against me? As many as seven times?'

[22]'I wouldn't say seven times,' replied Jesus. 'Why not – seventy times seven?'

[23]'So, you see,' he went on, 'the kingdom of heaven is like a royal personage who wanted to settle up accounts with his servants. [24]As he was beginning to sort it all out, one man was brought before him who owed ten thousand talents. [25]He had no means of paying it back, so the master ordered him to be sold, with his wife and children and everything he possessed, and payment to be made.

[26]'So the servant fell down and prostrated himself before the master.

'"Have mercy on me," he said, "and I'll pay you everything!"

[27]'The master was very sorry for the servant, and let him off. He forgave him the loan.

[28]'But that servant went out and found one of his fellow-servants, who owed him a hundred dinars. He seized him and began to throttle him. "Pay me back what you owe me!" he said.

[29]'The colleague fell down and begged him, "Have mercy on me, and I'll pay you!"

[30]'But he refused, and went and threw him into prison until he could pay the debt.

³¹'So when his fellow-servants saw what had happened, they were very upset. They went and informed their master about the whole affair. ³²Then his master summoned him.

'"You're a scoundrel of a servant!" he said to him. "I let you off the whole debt, because you begged me to. ³³Shouldn't you have taken pity on your colleague, like I took pity on you?"

³⁴'His master was angry, and handed him over to the torturers, until he had paid the whole debt. ³⁵And that's what my heavenly father will do to you, unless each of you forgives your brother or sister from your heart.'

There are at least three levels at which we should read this sharp and startling story. And at least three levels at which we should apply it to our lives, not least our lives in church.

Start, though, with Peter's question. It seems practical, almost common sense, but also a bit naive. Jesus has told us to forgive; very well, but supposing someone does the same bad thing again and again. Isn't there a limit? Wouldn't seven times be enough?

Some translations make out that Jesus said 'seventy-seven times'; but actually the word more likely means 'seventy times seven'. Four hundred and ninety! What's that about?

Jesus, of course, didn't mean that you should be counting up, through clenched teeth, so that on the four hundred and ninety-first time you could finally take revenge. If that was how you were thinking about it, it would show you'd never really forgiven once, let alone seven times or seventy times seven. So what was he meaning?

The story he tells takes us straight to the first level of meaning. If you yourself have been forgiven, then your gratitude for that ought to make you ready to forgive others. It's that straightforward. When someone annoys you – drives across in front of you when it was your right of way, takes your seat on the bus, or even, in church, sings loudly out of tune right behind you – then it's easy to allow it to fester. You may still be thinking about it a day or a week later. With larger annoyances it can go on for months or years. Your entire life can be blighted by these angry memories, by the sense of frustration and self-righteousness. How could they behave like that to me?

Jesus' first and best answer would be this. Just imagine what God and his angels think about what you did yesterday to the person you bumped into on the street when you weren't looking. Just think how many people may quite rightly be angry with you for your carelessness, your arrogance, your selfishness. And just think how the angels think about the way *you* sometimes sing in church. And yet you have been forgiven. When you say your prayers today, God isn't sitting there thinking crossly 'How dare you! I'm still angry with you after what you did last week!' He has forgiven you. Is it then too much to ask that you do the same?

Underneath that, there is a second level. My wife and I once had long conversations with a student who found herself incapable of feeling God's love. She believed in Jesus; she had prayed and read the Bible; but she couldn't feel a thing. She wanted to know God's love the way her friends said they did. But it wasn't happening. Eventually, as we talked about her life, it all came out. She hated her parents. She resented the sort of people they were, the way they'd treated her. So she had closed up her heart. Where there should have been an open readiness for God's love, there was a steel wall. It was as though you cut off the telephone line to stop certain people ringing you up and then grumbled because you couldn't phone your best friend. Forgiveness and love are a two-way street. The same part of you, spiritually, both gives and receives. If you shut down the part labelled 'forgiveness', you shut down the part labelled 'forgiveness' – in both directions. The ending of the story seems harsh. But at the level of psychological reality, it rings true.

The third level of meaning is altogether bigger, and goes back to the 'seventy times seven'. In the book of Daniel (9.24) the prophet is told, after praying that Jerusalem will be forgiven, that it will take 'seventy weeks of years' – in other words, seventy times seven years – before transgression, sin and iniquity are finally dealt with. This takes us back even further, to the ancient law of the Jubilee (Leviticus 25), which lays down that every forty-nine years (seven times seven) all debts must be remitted, with land returning to its original owners. Daniel is speaking of a Great Jubilee, a cosmic version of the Jubilee law. There will come a time when God will deal, once and for all, with all debts of every kind.

And Jesus? Well, Jesus announced that the moment had come. He was the Great Jubilee in person. His entire mission was about implementing God's age-old plan to deal with the evil that had infected the whole world. Forgiveness wasn't an incidental feature of his kingdom-movement. It was the name of the game. Those of us who find ourselves drawn into that movement must learn how to play that game, all the time. It's what we're about. It's what *God* is about.

Today

Loving Lord, teach us to forgive as we have been forgiven.

WEEK 4: SUNDAY

Psalm 23

¹The LORD is my shepherd, I shall not want.
    ²He makes me lie down in green pastures;
he leads me beside still waters;
        ³he restores my soul.
He leads me in right paths
    for his name's sake.
⁴Even though I walk through the darkest valley,
    I fear no evil;

71

for you are with me;
> your rod and your staff –
> they comfort me.
⁵You prepare a table before me
> in the presence of my enemies;
you anoint my head with oil;
> my cup overflows.
⁶Surely goodness and mercy shall follow me
> all the days of my life,
and I shall dwell in the house of the Lord
> my whole life long.

As I suggested earlier, farm animals are not as stupid as town-dwellers often imagine. They recognize individual faces – faces of other animals, faces of humans too. They know individual voices. They pick up signals and react accordingly. If it's someone they know or trust, they will be happy; if not, they may well be afraid. In this, perhaps the most famous Psalm in the book, the poet has managed, in the first four verses, to get right inside what we might call the mind of an animal – in this case, the sheep.

Sheep are very vulnerable. By themselves, they can't find the way to good pasture and drinking water. In the Middle East, these things are hard to find, and it's the shepherd's job to know where they are. That's quite a challenge in a region where, for much of the year, there is little rain. And there are dangers all around: dark crevasses where one could get lost, or stuck, or be at the mercy of robbers, wolves or lions.

From the sheep's-eye point of view, therefore, the shepherd brings a huge sigh of relief. I know this shepherd. I trust him. I'll be all right. When I follow him closely we always end up with good grass to eat and water to drink. We'll have to go on some odd paths from time to time but they always get us to the right place. And when danger approaches – well, the shepherd will look after us. He has a big stick and he knows how to use it. We'll be all right.

Many generations of devout Jews, from long before the time of Jesus to this day, have prayed that Psalm, putting themselves into the picture. Yahweh, Israel's God, was like that with them! They could trust him for everything, even when everything went dark. And now, many generations of Christians have prayed the Psalm in the same way, in the light of the many passages where Jesus picks up the shepherd-promise and applies it to himself. In fact, the gospel story is not unlike the picture of the shepherd and the sheep: Jesus leading his disciples around Galilee, teaching them, healing people as he goes. And as the story moves us forwards towards the valley of the shadow of death, we look on in awe and wonder as the Good Shepherd goes ahead of us into the darkness. His rod and his staff, two poles of wood, come together in a new pattern, a shape which will etch itself on the heart of the world. We look at the cross and we are comforted.

The poem then shifts, in the last two verses, away from the sheep and the shepherd. Once we come out of the dark shadow, we become human in a new way. A table is spread before us, despite the people who still mock us and try to attack us for our faith and our hope. God provides us with good things of all sorts. Instead of the sheep who are led to food and drink, we become people who, strengthened by God's food, discover that he is gently following them in the new ventures to which they are called. 'Goodness and mercy', or in another translation 'kindness and faithful love', will follow us. That is to say, God himself will follow us – and God, as we constantly need to remind ourselves, is himself overflowing with goodness, kindness, mercy and faithful love.

Again the poem shifts. For the original poet, 'dwelling in the Lord's house for ever' would mean, literally, making one's home in the Temple in Jerusalem. But already within ancient Judaism 'the Lord's house' had come to mean, by extension, the places where his people met to pray, and the holy book they studied wherever they went. The first Christians believed that the Temple itself had been transformed from being made of stone, timber, bricks and mortar to being made of flesh, blood and bones: Jesus' flesh and blood, where the living God truly and utterly dwelt, and then, astonishingly, the human bodies of his followers, as God's Spirit came to live within them. We make this poem our own, then, confident that Jesus, the good shepherd, will do all that the first four verses claim. Confident, too, that his dwelling in us and ours in him, rooted as they are in his kindness and mercy, will never come to an end.

Today

Lord, we thank you for your faithful love and mercy. Look after us each moment, we pray, and lead us where we need to go.

WEEK 4: MONDAY

Matthew 19; focused on 19.16–26

[16]Suddenly a man came up to Jesus. 'Teacher,' he asked, 'what good thing must I do if I'm to possess the life of the age to come?'

[17]'Why come to me with questions about what's good?' retorted Jesus. 'There is one who is good! If you want to enter into life, keep the commandments.'

[18]'Which ones?' he asked.

'These ones,' Jesus answered: '"don't murder, don't commit adultery, don't steal, don't tell lies under oath, [19]respect your father and mother", and "love your neighbour as yourself".'

[20]'I've kept the lot,' said the young man. 'What am I still short of?'

[21]'If you want to complete the set,' Jesus replied, 'go and sell everything you own and give it to the poor. That way you'll have treasure in heaven! Then come and follow me.'

[22]When the young man heard him say that, he went away very sad. He had many possessions.

²³Jesus said to his disciples, 'I'm telling you the truth: it's very hard for a rich person to get into the kingdom of heaven. ²⁴Let me say it again: it's easier for a camel to go through the eye of a needle than for a rich person to enter God's kingdom.'

²⁵The disciples were completely flabbergasted when they heard that. 'So who then can be saved?' they asked.

²⁶Jesus looked round at them. 'Humanly speaking,' he replied, 'it's impossible. But everything's possible with God.'

At the time I am writing this, a politician has just received loud and long applause for saying rude words about the very rich, especially people in the banks who pay themselves vast sums of money. Everybody likes to hate the rich. That's the popular mood right now.

That's why the most surprising thing about this story is – how surprised the disciples were when Jesus declared it would be hard for the rich to enter God's kingdom (verse 24). You might have thought that would be obvious, not least to someone who had been listening to Jesus and following him for some time. But it seems as though the disciples still looked at the world through the lens which said that the more rich you were, the more God was pleased with you. Some passages in scripture do seem to point that way. But mostly this was an assumption people made, a way of coming to terms with the obvious inequalities in society.

(Let's be clear, by the way. When the rich man speaks of 'having eternal life', and when Jesus speaks of 'entering the kingdom of heaven', or 'having treasure in heaven', they are not talking about 'life after death' in the popular, modern sense. They are talking about the whole new world that they believed God was going to make, 'the renewal of all things' (verse 28). The point is that they believed that 'heaven' was going to rule on earth, so that the question was about who would inherit and share in that new heaven-and-earth world.)

Jesus had seen, in this case and no doubt many others, that earthly riches form a lining of lead around the heart. They insulate you from God and from other people. They drag you down to be less and less the person you might have become. Here was this man, all eager and willing – except for the one thing that mattered.

Jesus' initial reply is also quite surprising. He lists the commandments, but not all of them: murder, adultery, theft, lying, honouring father and mother, and (an ancient summary of the whole law which Jesus had made his own) loving your neighbour as yourself. What about the earlier commandments, the ones about not having or making any other gods but Israel's God, the one about honouring his name, and the command about the Sabbath? Wouldn't we have expected Jesus to include those too?

Well, there is a sense in which he does. When the man tells him he has observed all those commandments, Jesus gives him two more: sell your possessions and give the money to the poor, and come and follow me. In the place where we might have expected Jesus to speak about putting God first, getting rid of idols, and honouring God's name, we have the command to get rid of money and to follow Jesus. This makes us realize that when Jesus challenged the man at the beginning ('Why ask me about what's good? There is only one who is good') there may have been more to the quip than meets the eye. Putting Jesus first and putting God first seem to be coming close to the same thing.

That's why we can never remain content with shallow discussions about the goodies and baddies in today's culture. Yes, some people play fast and loose with other people's money and get fat on the proceeds. But plenty in the same profession work tirelessly for their customers and give away much of their own income. Yes, many people in the western world today have made greed a way of life. But many work responsibly within the system and do their best to make it more humane, more honouring to God. All Christians should ask themselves, on a regular basis, if there is anything holding them back from following Jesus completely and utterly, any lead weights around part of their character or lifestyle. Who knows what the answer will be? All we know is that, when the answer comes, it will be fully in line with the scriptures upon which Jesus was drawing, and even more fully in line with Jesus himself.

In the last analysis, it's all down to God's power. In the previous chapter, we were taught to forgive because God had forgiven us. Here we are taught that the way to follow the God of all power and possibility may well be to give away our own power and possibilities. When God finally transforms all things, then and only then will we discover who his true disciples have been.

Today

Lord, make us grateful for all you give us, and ready to give it all back to you.

WEEK 4: TUESDAY

Matthew 20; focused on 20.1–16

[1]'So you see,' Jesus continued, 'the kingdom of heaven is like a landowner who went out early in the morning to hire workers for his vineyard. [2]He agreed with the workers to give them a pound a day, and sent them off to his vineyard.

[3]'He went out again in the middle of the morning, and saw some others standing in the marketplace with nothing to do.

[4]'"You too can go to the vineyard," he said, "and I'll give you what's right." [5]So off they went.

'He went out again about midday, and then in the middle of the afternoon, and did the same. [6]Then, with only an hour of the day left, he went out and found other people standing there.

'"Why are you standing here all day with nothing to do?" he asked them.

⁷'"Because no one has hired us," they replied.

'"Well," he said, "you too can go into the vineyard."

⁸'When evening came, the vineyard-owner said to his servant, "Call the workers and give them their pay. Start with the last, and go on to the first."

⁹'So the ones who had worked for one hour came, and each of them received a pound. ¹⁰When the first ones came, they thought they would get something more; but they, too, each received a pound.

¹¹'When they had been given it, they grumbled against the landowner. ¹²"This lot who came in last", they said, "have only worked for one hour – and they've been put on a level with us! And we did all the hard work, all day, and in the heat as well!"

¹³'"My friend," he said to one of them, "I'm not doing you any wrong. You agreed with me on one pound, didn't you? ¹⁴Take it! It's yours! And be on your way. I want to give this fellow who came at the end the same as you. ¹⁵Or are you suggesting that I'm not allowed to do what I like with my own money? Or are you giving me the evil eye because I'm good?"

¹⁶'So those at the back will be at the front, and the front ones at the back.'

The game was nearly over, and neither side had scored a goal. The spectators were getting angry, and the players were exhausted. One player on the home team, in particular, had worked tirelessly the whole game, running from end to end, always in the right place, wearing himself out to stop the opposition getting through, then launching counter-attacks. Again and again he gave of his best, but the rest of the team couldn't translate his efforts into an actual score.

With five minutes to go, the manager decided to try something desperate. He took the key player off, and brought on as a substitute a fresh, bright young man who had only played one or two games at the top level. Almost at once the ball came his way. With devil-may-care youthful energy he weaved his way through the defence and scored a great goal. The crowd went wild. The opposition caved in. The game was soon over.

The young man was cheered to the echo, carried around the stadium by happy fans. Eventually the older player, who had worked so hard throughout almost all the game, came out to join the party. A mixture of emotions. He had done all the hard work, and the other man, who had done none of it, had got all the glory.

That's the story Jesus told, only in a different setting. We don't so often have day-labourers lining up, waiting all day to be hired, and then paid at the boss's whim. But what is the story about?

It illustrates what Jesus had just said, which he was to repeat at the end: many who are first will be last, and the last first. As so often, this has at least three levels of meaning which we should explore.

To begin with, Jesus was facing his followers with the fact that God remains sovereign over his whole kingdom-project. Nobody can claim a special place either because they've worked hard, or because they've given up so much, or because they were in it from the beginning. This is a warning to the disciples themselves, who, as Jesus' closest friends and associates, might well have supposed that they were going to retain the top jobs in whatever future God had in store. Jesus does indeed indicate that they will have special places (19.28) – though since he mentions the twelve of them, and since we know that Judas then defected, we should be careful not to build too much on that either. Later on in the chapter the disciples show how much they need this lesson, as James and John try to make sure they are the first in line.

But, second, the message goes wider, right across Matthew's gospel, in relation to the place of the Jewish people within God's larger purposes. Jesus has made it clear, two or three times, that ancient Israel has a priority. He has honoured that. As St Paul says, the gospel is 'to the Jew first'. But the gospel is not only for Jews. As Paul goes on, '– and for Gentiles also'. That was bad enough for the pious Jew to contemplate. But now there was a sense, following some of Jesus' earlier sayings, that the 'obvious' people had had to go to the back of the queue. This was not only humiliating. It might have looked as though God had changed his mind.

Jesus was quite clear. God hasn't changed his mind. It was always his plan to humble the exalted and exalt the humbled.

The third level, then, reaches out to us in our life of faith today. Our western 'celebrity' culture favours those who manage to push themselves to the front, whether it's the people with the most obvious talents or the stars with the sharpest agents. Sadly, that can spill over into the life of the church: famous preachers and leaders get attention and the 'ordinary' Christian becomes a passive spectator. We need, again and again, to learn that there are no such people as 'ordinary' Christians. In the 'renewal of all things' which Jesus spoke about (19.28), all sorts of people will stand out as the real heroes and heroines of faith, though nobody has ever heard of them before. They will be the ones who, whether for five minutes or fifty years, served God with total and glad obedience, giving themselves completely to holiness, prayer, and works of love and mercy. Such people are the pure gold of the church. But, as so often, gold remains hidden and takes some finding.

Today

Gracious Lord, help us to be humble enough to take whatever place we are given, and zealous enough to work wholeheartedly for your glory where and when you call us.

WEEK 4: WEDNESDAY
Matthew 21.1–22; focused on 21.1–17

[1]When they came near to Jerusalem, and arrived at Bethphage on the Mount of Olives, Jesus sent two of the disciples on ahead.

[2]'Go into the village over there,' he said, 'and at once you'll find a donkey tied up, and a foal beside it. Untie them and bring them to me. [3]And if anyone says anything to you, say, "The Master needs them."'

He sent them off at once.

[4]This happened so that the prophet's words might be fulfilled:

[5]Tell this to Zion's daughter:
Look now! Here comes your king;
He's humble, mounted on an ass,
Yes, on a foal, its young.

[6]So the disciples went off and did as Jesus had told them.

[7]They brought the donkey and its foal, and put their cloaks on them, and Jesus sat on them.

[8]The huge crowd spread their cloaks on the road. Others cut branches from the trees and scattered them on the road. [9]The crowds who went on ahead of him, and those who were following behind, shouted out,

Hosanna now to David's Son!
God's blessing on the coming one!
Hosanna in the highest!

[10]When they came into Jerusalem, the whole city was gripped with excitement.

'Who is this?' they were saying.

[11]'This is the prophet, Jesus,' replied the crowds, 'from Nazareth in Galilee!'

[12]Jesus went into the Temple and threw out all the people who were buying and selling in the Temple. He upturned

the tables of the money-changers and the seats of the dove-sellers.

[13]'This is what the Bible says,' he said to them,

My house will be called a house of prayer –
But you have made it a brigands' lair!'

[14]The blind and the lame came to him in the Temple, and he healed them. [15]But when the chief priests and the scribes saw the remarkable things he was doing, and the children shouting out 'Hosanna to David's son!' in the Temple, they were very cross.

[16]'Do you hear what they're saying?' they asked Jesus.

'Yes,' said Jesus. 'Did you never read what it says,

You called forth praise to rise to you
From newborn babes and infants too!

[17]Then he left them, and went out of the city to Bethany, where he stayed the night.

We reach Palm Sunday in Matthew's story ten days before we get there in our own Lenten journey. It's just as well. There is so much packed between Palm Sunday and Good Friday that it's important to get advance notice of what's in store.

It is one of the great scenes in all scripture. Jesus riding into Jerusalem on a donkey: it could be the climax of an opera, or a Shakespeare play. For Matthew, though, it's the climax of a much longer and more complicated story: the whole story of God and Israel. And it turns out that the play, at the moment, anyway, is more of a tragedy than a comedy.

St John put it like this: he came to his own, and his own didn't receive him. All along Jesus had made it clear that his particular vocation was to present the arrival of heaven's kingdom to the people of Israel. Having prepared the way by his work up in the north, he has now arrived, with a great throng of Passover pilgrims, at the holy city itself.

Only it wasn't as holy as it should have been. Jerusalem, the city chosen by God as his own resting-place, had also been chosen by many as their place of profit. The first time I went into the Old City of Jerusalem, the first sign I saw was a money-changer's shop. I suspect it's always been like that, with people from all over the world needing now to use the local currency. In the case of the Temple, of course, pilgrims needed to buy animals for sacrifice. Much safer that way than bringing a lamb or a goat from far off, to risk it being savaged by predators on the way. Come with cash, change it locally, buy a pure animal on site ready for sacrifice. Simple. And the local traders did well out of it.

But Jesus' protest against the Temple wasn't just about it being, in that sense, 'a den of robbers'. He was quoting the prophet Jeremiah at that point, and Jeremiah wasn't just worried about economic exploitation. Something deeper and darker was afoot. Behind all the outward trappings of the Temple, Jesus could see that the whole place, and the whole city, had come to symbolize the determination of Israel to do things their own way; in particular, to embrace a vision of God and God's kingdom which was fundamentally different from the vision which he was announcing and living out. Their vision would have climaxed in a Messiah coming on a war-horse. Jesus' vision led him to act out the prophecy of Zechariah: your king is coming to you, humble, and mounted on a donkey. This simple yet profound symbolic action continues to resonate out into the world where, even among people who profess to follow Jesus, the war-horse is still preferred to the donkey.

The third level concerns what Matthew is saying about Jesus himself. The local crowds, seeing all the commotion as Jesus came into the city, were told by the pilgrims that 'this is the prophet Jesus, from Nazareth in Galilee' (verse 11). But

Matthew makes it clear that, though Jesus is indeed a prophet, he is much more. To begin with, he is the 'Son of David' – the royal title which so annoyed the chief priests and scribes (verse 15). They were perhaps frightened of what the Roman authorities might do to the city if it welcomed a would-be king. They may also have been frightened of what a would-be king and his followers might say about them.

Things don't stop there. The Temple was, after all, the place where the one true God was supposed to live on earth with his people. For Matthew (1.23; 28.20), Jesus himself has become that place. In this scene, we discover the great truth that the early Christians embraced and developed: that the old Temple on Mount Zion was simply a signpost, pointing forwards to the new reality of God's presence with his people.

Jerusalem, then, wasn't big enough for Jesus and the Temple together. They were bound to clash. That clash begins the sequence of events which will lead, soon enough, to Jesus' death. But, as we watch, we also see the signs of what that death might mean. If Jesus is the true Temple, we might expect that it is in him, rather than in the Temple, that healing and forgiveness are to be found. Matthew draws our attention to the odd fact that 'the blind and the lame came to him in the Temple, and he cured them'. In 1 Samuel 5.8, the blind and the lame had been excluded from the Temple, following the orders of David himself. Now the Son of David likewise keeps the Temple free from the blind and the lame – by healing them. It would be hard to sum up any better the difference between what Jesus was offering and what his contemporaries were wanting.

Today

Gracious Lord, challenge us when we distort your will and your promise, and come to dwell with us and in us now and for ever.

WEEK 4: THURSDAY

Matthew 21.23–46; focused on 21.33–45

[33]'Listen to another parable,' Jesus went on. 'Once upon a time there was a householder who planted a vineyard, built a wall for it, dug out a wine-press in it, and built a tower. Then he let it out to tenant farmers and went away on a journey.

[34]'When harvest time arrived, he sent his slaves to the farmers to collect his produce. [35]The farmers seized his slaves; they beat one, killed another, and stoned another. [36]Again he sent other slaves, more than before, and they treated them in the same way. [37]Finally he sent his son to them.

'"They'll respect my son," he said.

[38]'But the farmers saw the son.

'"This fellow's the heir!" they said to themselves. "Come on, let's kill him, and then we can take over the property!"

[39]'So they seized him, threw him out of the vineyard, and killed him.

[40]'Now then: when the vineyard-owner returns, what will he do to those farmers?'

[41]'He'll kill them brutally, the wretches!' they said. 'And he'll lease the vineyard to other farmers who'll give him the produce at the right time.'

[42]'Did you never read what the Bible says?' said Jesus to them:

The stone the builders threw away
Is now atop the corner;
It's from the Lord, all this, they say
And we looked on in wonder.

[43]'So let me tell you this: God's kingdom is going to be taken away from you and given to a nation that will produce the goods. [44]Anyone who falls on this stone will be smashed to pieces, and anyone it falls on will be crushed.'

[45]When the chief priests and the Pharisees heard his parables, they knew he was talking about them.

I was taking a service in a local church when this passage was the second reading. Over at the side of the church was a family with a three-year-old boy who appeared to be playing with his toys, taking no notice of the service. But when the reader finished this parable, about the wicked tenants who beat up the owner's messengers and finally kill his son, there was a momentary pause; and, in the silence, the boy's voice stood out loud and clear: 'That's not a very nice story!'

Well, no, it isn't, and that's part of the point. We come to the gospels hoping and imagining that they are going to be 'nice'; that we will find a Jesus who tells us it's all right, we don't have to worry, nobody's going to get hurt, no one will even be cross. But with the world the way it is, if God doesn't get cross about it he is not a good God. If he doesn't do something about it, sooner or later, he's quite simply not God.

The whole New Testament is based on the belief that in Jesus of Nazareth the living God took the world into his hands at last in judgment and mercy. When I say 'took it into his hands', there are various different meanings there, which have to be explored in due course. Tragically, it was God's own people, Jesus' own people, Israel itself that stood in the way of what God was wanting to do.

In the Bible, the 'vineyard' is often used as an image for the people of Israel. In the old prophets, the vineyard has often gone wrong, gone wild, rebelled against its planter. In this story, though, it's the tenants who are at fault. The 'vineyard' itself seems to be God's inner purpose, Israel as the bearer of his saving plan for the world. As in the Old Testament, God sent prophets to his people, but his people refused to listen. Now at last he is sending his son – and his people, instead of listening, think that if they kill the son they can have the vineyard for themselves.

This is at the heart of it. Jesus' challenge to Israel – that it was time at last for God to become king, and that this was happening through him and his work – was too much. As with the young man two chapters earlier, his contemporaries couldn't match the total demand of God's kingdom. And, to explain the result, Jesus called on other biblical images: the stone that won't fit the wall but will go nicely at the very top (Psalm 118.22–23), and the stone that will crush all opposition (Daniel 2.34). The English words 'son' and 'stone' are very similar; in the same way the Hebrew words *ben* (son) and *eben* (stone) are very much alike. The rejected son, like the rejected stone, will become the Lord of all and judge of all.

This parable is Jesus' own explanation for what was happening. Once again, telling cryptic stories is the only way you can say the really important things. As we watch, we find ourselves drawn into the action. Are we part of the group that don't want the Owner to take control of his own vineyard? Would we rather keep it for ourselves?

Today

Almighty God, give us grace to produce the fruits of your kingdom, that we may celebrate your Son, the chief cornerstone of your new Temple.

WEEK 4: FRIDAY

Matthew 22; focused on 22.1–14

[1]Jesus spoke to them once again in parables.

[2]'The kingdom of heaven', he said, 'is like a king who made a wedding feast for his son. [3]He sent his slaves to call the invited guests to the wedding, and they didn't want to come.

[4]'Again he sent other slaves, with these instructions: "Say to the guests, Look! I've got my dinner ready; my bulls and fatted calves have been killed; everything is prepared. Come to the wedding!"

[5]'But they didn't take any notice. They went off, one to his own farm, another to see to his business. [6]The others laid hands on his slaves, abused them and killed them. [7](The king

87

was angry, and sent his soldiers to destroy those murderers and burn down their city.) [8]Then he said to his slaves, "The wedding is ready, but the guests didn't deserve it. [9]So go to the roads leading out of town, and invite everyone you find to the wedding." [10]The slaves went off into the streets and rounded up everyone they found, bad and good alike. And the wedding was filled with partygoers.

[11]'But when the king came in to look at the guests, he saw there a man who wasn't wearing a wedding suit.

[12]'"My friend," he said to him, "how did you get in here without a wedding suit?" And he was speechless. [13]Then the king said to the servants, "Tie him up, hands and feet, and throw him into the darkness outside, where people weep and grind their teeth."

[14]'Many are called, you see, but few are chosen.'

'Get me to the church on time!' It's a famous song from a famous musical. I suspect it's a favourite because we've all been to weddings, we all remember the sense of occasion, of dressing up, of this being the bride's and the groom's big day and everyone wanting to be there on time in proper order to give them an occasion to remember. Even in our own day in the western world, where marriage has been knocked about so much by careless pseudo-morality, and the divorce rate has risen alarmingly, almost everybody knows in their bones that this is something to celebrate, something to do properly.

In the ancient world, especially in the ancient Jewish world where the sense of family had remained very strong, this was even more so. And if the king himself had invited you to the wedding of his son . . . well, then you would be planning for months what to wear, what gift to bring, how to make sure everything was right on the day.

All this only heightens the sense of shock, disappointment and anger at the story Jesus now tells. He exaggerates the detail to make it lurid, almost surreal. The guests, finally summoned, beat up and kill the slaves sent with the invitation, and the king

WEEK 4: FRIDAY Matthew 22

sends troops to burn their city. But then comes the second shock. The king sends out some more slaves, and invites all and sundry to come to the party. In they come, 'good and bad' alike (there are echoes here of the 'good and bad' fish found in the Great Net of 13.48). Clearly the larger implications of the parable are influencing quite dramatically the way the original story is being told.

The new guests may have made it on time, but they are not all properly dressed. Here again the story has taken a lurid turn. One guest has not put on the wedding robe, and is thrown into the outer darkness. By this stage it's clear that, as with Psalm 23 which we looked at last Sunday, the original picture has more or less disappeared, and we are left with a more direct statement. The king has now invited the whole world to the wedding party originally planned for Israel. But those who attend as part of this suddenly enlarged guest-list must take care to turn up in the proper outfit.

We should not be surprised that some people have tried to suggest that Jesus never told this parable, or that this last bit was added later on. You can go to extraordinary lengths to protect your image of the gentle Jesus who wouldn't hurt a fly. But what he is saying, as he does in one way or another throughout, is that just because God's wedding party has been thrown open to all and sundry – to Gentiles as well as Jews, as Paul never tired of insisting – that doesn't mean that once they've accepted the invitation they can carry on as though it wasn't *God's* wedding party. All are welcome; but all must dress appropriately.

Today

Almighty Father, give us the joy of accepting your invitation, and the wisdom to dress in the right way for the party.

WEEK 4: SATURDAY
Matthew 23; focused on 23.29–39

[29]'Woe betide you, scribes and Pharisees, you hypocrites! You build the tombs of the prophets, and you decorate the memorials of the righteous, [30]and you say, "If we'd lived in the days of our ancestors, we wouldn't have gone along with them in killing the prophets." [31]So you testify against yourselves that you are the children of the people who murdered the prophets! [32]Well then, go ahead: complete the work your ancestors began! [33]You snakes, you nest of vipers, how can you escape the judgment of Gehenna? [34]Because of all this,' Jesus concluded, 'I'm sending you prophets, wise and learned people. Some of them you will kill and crucify. Some of them you will whip in your synagogues. You'll chase them from town to town. [35]That's how all the righteous blood that's been shed on earth, from the blood of righteous Abel to the blood of Zechariah son of Barachiah (you murdered him between sanctuary and altar) – all that blood will come upon you. [36]I'm telling you the solemn truth: it will all come on this generation.

[37]'Jerusalem, Jerusalem, killing the prophets and stoning those who are sent to you! How often have I longed to gather up your children, the way a hen gathers up her brood under her wings, and you didn't want me to! [38]Now, see here: your house has been abandoned by God; it's a ruin. [39]Yes, I tell you: you won't see me again from now on until you say, "Welcome in the name of the Lord!"'

We stood in the autumn light beside the huge waterfall, mesmerized by the sheer volume of water pouring over and crashing down on the rocks beneath, unable to hear ourselves speak because of the rush and roar of the turbulent river. Then, as we walked back up the path to where we'd parked the car, we thought of all the tiny streams we'd seen earlier in the day, tinkling along gently high in the hills, and how each one had contributed to the massive flood we had just witnessed.

Down they come into the valley, each making its way and lending its weight to the wide, powerful river.

Something of that same sense, of thousands of different streams each contributing to an eventual waterfall, is contained here, as Jesus concludes his solemn denunciation of both the official and the self-appointed guardians of Israel's ancestral traditions. Jesus looked back, up into the far hills of Israel's history, and saw a long line of prophets and righteous people who had been rejected by the leaders and opinion-formers of their day. Again and again it had happened. Little by little the streams have grown into a flood; and now Jesus sees the present leaders, his own contemporaries, flowing along in the same tradition. Right back as far as Abel, the first murdered man, right on to the more recent prophet Zechariah son of Barachiah, Israel's leaders have rejected and killed those who were sent to them; and now they are doing the same one more time.

What Jesus can see as well, though, is that there is a great waterfall just ahead. All this weight of water will not simply stop when it comes to the cliff: it will crash over it, thundering down to the depths. A mighty disaster is on the way. Many others had warned of similar things; Jesus, like the prophet he was, can see it only too clearly. And when it happens it won't be arbitrary. It won't be an accident. It will be the direct result of all these small streams of rebellion coming together into the greatest rebellion of them all.

But that isn't the end of the story. In the middle of the warning, Jesus speaks of his own longing to do something about it. God has indeed abandoned the Temple to its fate (verse 38). But, like a mother hen gathering the chickens under her wing to protect them against a fire, or a fox, Jesus has longed to gather Jerusalem and its people to himself so that he could take upon himself the full force of the coming disaster. Somehow, as we go through the next four chapters of Matthew's gospel, we need to remember that we are watching two different scenes: God's judgment on his rebellious people, and Jesus standing in the way, offering to take that judgment upon himself.

Today

Lord Jesus, Messiah and King, help us to stand in awe at your solemn words, and in gratitude at your offer of rescue.

WEEK 5: SUNDAY

Psalm 130

[1]Out of the depths I cry to you, O LORD.
    [2]Lord, hear my voice!
Let your ears be attentive
    to the voice of my supplications!
[3]If you, O LORD, should mark iniquities,
    Lord, who could stand?
[4]But there is forgiveness with you,
    so that you may be revered.
[5]I wait for the LORD, my soul waits,
    and in his word I hope;
[6]my soul waits for the Lord
    more than those who watch for the morning,
    more than those who watch for the morning.
[7]O Israel, hope in the LORD!
    For with the LORD there is steadfast love,
    and with him is great power to redeem.
[8]It is he who will redeem Israel
    from all its iniquities.

The deep distress we sense as we read this Psalm has, paradoxically perhaps, given great hope to millions down the years. No matter how deep we have sunk, no matter what sorrows or tragedies we may encounter, the Psalms have been there before us. Not only do they encourage us to believe that we have not, after all, fallen off the map. They give us words so that, when our own words fail to do justice to our misery, they will do instead.

The Psalm doesn't hide. There's no point pretending, putting a brave face on it before God. (By the way, if you're reading this Psalm today in a bright, cheerful mood, pray it on behalf of the many for whom today is dark and sorrowful.) 'Out of the depths!' That's how it is, for all of us some of the time, for some of us most of the time. Let's tell it like it is.

Worse: the poet has a sense that somehow it's his own fault. When disaster strikes and it's someone else's fault, we can gain some relief by blaming them, perhaps hoping for justice. But when it's my own fault, even in part, the blame turns back on me. That is the road to the deepest depths of all, where we are not only miserable but feel guilty. Depression often takes the form, as a medical friend once said to me, of putting ourselves on trial and acting as judge, jury and chief prosecution witness all rolled into one. We then lock ourselves in the dungeon of our own misery and throw away the key.

It is out of that sense of helpless and hopeless sadness that the poem cries out: Lord, hear my voice! Listen! If you keep a record of wrongdoing, we'd all be in deep trouble; but what you offer is forgiveness! That's why we worship you! The news of forgiveness, of a free pardon, is the best news of all. The lock is broken; the prison door stands open; we are free to go.

It hasn't happened yet. The Psalm ends with redemption, forgiveness, still in the future. Yet the strong affirmation of God's forgiving kindness in verse 4 is the anchor which then, despite all, holds us upright. Then it's a matter of hope and patience: 'waiting', three times repeated in verses 5 and 6, is where it's at. 'Lord, give me patience,' says the T-shirt, 'and I want it right now!' But what matters here is the waiting, the settled concentration on God's word which alone assures us that there is hope because God is gracious.

As we journey through Lent, all sorts of things may have come up to test us, to make us despair. There is some way still to go, but we know who it is we're following. By the end of the Psalm, the poet is strong enough to commend to the whole nation the path of patience he himself is treading. 'O Israel, hope in the Lord; with the Lord there is steadfast love; he has great power to redeem.' He doesn't say what form the rescue will take. He only knows who it is that will provide it.

Today

Gracious Lord, when we are in the depths, come to us with your mercy and assure us of your power to rescue. And give us the patience to wait for you to do it.

WEEK 5: MONDAY

Matthew 24; focused on 24.15–28

[15]"So when you see "the sacrilege that desolates", as Daniel the prophet put it, standing in the holy place (the reader should understand), [16]then those who are in Judaea should take to their heels and run to the mountains. [17]If you're up on your roof, don't go down into the house to get things out. [18]If you're in the fields, don't go back to pick up your cloak. [19]It's going to be terrible for pregnant and nursing women during those days. [20]Pray that it won't be winter when you have to run away, or for that matter a sabbath. [21]Yes: there's going to be such great suffering then as has never been since the start of the world until now – no, and won't ever be again. [22]And if those days had not been shortened, nobody at all would have been rescued. But for the sake of God's chosen ones those days will be shortened.

[23]"Then if anyone says to you, "Look! Here is the Messiah!" or "Look! There he is!", don't believe them. [24]False messiahs will arise, you see, and false prophets too. They will provide great signs and portents, so as to deceive even God's chosen ones, if that were possible. [25]Remember, I'm telling you this beforehand!

> [26]'So if someone says to you, "Look! He's out in the wilderness", don't go out. If they say, "Look, he's in the inner room", don't believe them. [27]You see, the royal appearing of the son of man will be like the lightning that comes from the east and flashes across to the west. [28]Where the carcass is, there the vultures will gather.'

Browsing in an old library the other day, I came upon a book of cartoons from the late nineteenth century. They were political satires, commenting on the affairs of state of the time. Several different politicians were lampooned; all sorts of issues were obviously 'hot' at the time, with new laws some didn't like, the possibility of an unpopular war, and so on.

That much I could understand. But beyond that I couldn't go. I'm not a nineteenth-century historian, and I needed one right then to explain to me why this politician was drawn as a bird and that one as a zebra; why that particular law was unpopular; who was advocating the war, and who was resisting it. Several of the cartoons I couldn't even begin to understand. They had obviously been important in their own day, and would have had an instant impact. But without help I couldn't make head or tail of them.

Something of that same feeling of helplessness when faced with other people's symbols and images comes over us when we read ancient texts like Matthew 24 (which we do twice, today and tomorrow). What is the 'desolating sacrilege'? Who are these people who have to run away? What are these false prophets? What on earth is 'the coming of the Son of Man'?

Fortunately help is at hand. At the beginning of the chapter Matthew has made it clear that this is Jesus' answer to a double question. At the heart of it is Jesus' own solemn prophecy (verse 2) that the Temple is to be destroyed. We might have guessed from his action in driving out the money-changers that, like Jeremiah half a millennium earlier, he was denouncing the Temple and prophesying its fall, just as in the previous chapter he had denounced the Pharisees and warned of their imminent judgment. And, frankly, it didn't take much insight to see that if Jesus' contemporaries went on plotting and scheming against the power of Rome, sooner or later Rome would lose patience and send in the troops. So the disciples asked him when all this would happen – and what would be the sign of his 'coming', his royal enthronement, and of 'the close of the age', a cryptic way of saying 'the time when God finally does what he's promised and makes all things new'.

The difference between Jesus' prophecy of these forth-coming events and the speculations of his contemporaries was that he had a sense of his own role, his own fate, his own future being somehow bound up with it all. He wasn't just a spectator, a voice warning of danger. He was the one around whom Israel's God was re-ordering his people. He was the reality to which the Temple had pointed, the place and the means of God dwelling in person among his people. And he, like many others in his time, believed that this was the moment for the prophecies of Daniel to come true. Pagan hordes would place a blasphemous object in the Temple. Their armies would sweep through the holy land, and there would be no point in trying to hide in Jerusalem in the mistaken belief that it couldn't fall. The only solution would be to get out and run. And, in and through it all, there would be the 'coming' of the 'Son of Man'. Not his 'return', as many have supposed; as in Daniel, the 'coming' is his coming to God in vindication. He will be exalted; the Temple will be destroyed.

All these things, Matthew undoubtedly believed, took place within a generation. Jesus was exalted as sovereign over all (28.19); the Temple was destroyed in AD 70. But wise readers ever since have seen this specific prophecy as resonating out in wider circles. One day there will be an even greater moment of judgment and mercy, at the time Jesus called 'the renewal of all things' (19.28). Pondering and praying our way through the turbulent first century can give us a clue to how we should be, faithful and prayerful, in our own day and beyond.

Today

Make us, gracious Lord, faithful and patient as events unfold around us, always eager to shelter in your protection and celebrate your victory.

WEEK 5: TUESDAY
Matthew 24; focused on 24.45–51

[45]'So,' Jesus went on, 'who's going to play the part of the trustworthy and sensible slave, the one the master will set over his household, so that he will give them their meals at the right time? [46]It's good news for the servant whom the master finds doing just that when he comes. [47]I'm telling you the truth: he'll promote him to be over all his belongings. [48]But if the wicked slave says in his heart, "My master's taking his time", [49]and starts to beat the other slaves, and to feast and drink with the drunkards, [50]the master of that slave will come on a day he doesn't expect, and at a time he doesn't know. [51]He will cut him in two, and put him along with the hypocrites, where people will weep and grind their teeth.'

I vividly remember my first experience of working on a building site. I was a student, earning some money during the vacation. The work was physically hard – or rather, it would have been if we had kept it up all day. There was an unwritten law that you went at your tasks as slowly as you could, pausing regularly for a rest or a 'smoke break', except when the boss showed up. Then, of course, everyone would look brisk and get on as fast as they could. The play-acting would have been comic if the deceit hadn't been so distasteful.

Clearly, from Jesus' comments about the slaves doing their jobs while the master is away, this culture of working only when someone is watching is hardly a modern invention. Jesus is addressing his close followers, warning them of a coming time when they will have to get on with their work, staying faithful to him in his absence. They will have to look after his 'household' whether they think he'll be coming back the next minute or not.

The challenge to wait, and behave appropriately, during a long time of 'delay' (verse 48) was not a new one in Jesus' day. The Jews of the previous centuries had spoken of it constantly. They encouraged one another to stay faithful to their God, and to his covenant with them expressed in the Mosaic law, while they waited for God to act, to return to them in power, to rescue them from their enemies and set up his kingdom.

Jesus has taken this well-known theme and transformed it so that it applies more directly and vividly to his own followers after his approaching death. He knows that there will come a time of vindication. But nobody except God knows when that will be (verse 36). But he also knows that those who wait patiently, and get on with their tasks of looking after God's people, will be rewarded – and that those who don't will be punished.

This is a severe warning for all Christian leaders and teachers. Sometimes people seem to suppose that it doesn't really matter how you behave, that we can keep the wheels of the church turning all right without paying too much attention to the teaching of Jesus himself or the doctrine and lifestyle taught by his first followers. That attitude is then held in place by a sneering rejection of all talk of a future judgment. Such talk, it seems, fell out of fashion some time ago, and we can keep it that way (people seem to think) by telling horror-stories about old fire-and-brimstone preachers trying to scare people into good behaviour, or even into heaven. But just because people have overstated things in one direction, that doesn't mean there isn't a danger of overstatement in the other direction. If Lent is a time of reflection, penitence and discipline for all Christians, perhaps it is especially so for those who dare to think of themselves as slaves in charge of part of Jesus' household.

Today

Lord, as you have called us to your service, make us mindful and worthy of our calling.

WEEK 5: WEDNESDAY
Matthew 25; focused on 25.14–30

[14]'This is what it will be like,' Jesus went on. 'It will be like a man who was going off on a journey. He summoned his slaves, and handed over control of his property to them. [15]He gave five talents to the first, two to the next, and one to the last – each according to his ability. Then he left.

'Straight away [16]the man who had been given the five talents went out and traded with them, and made five more. [17]Similarly, the one who had received two talents went and made another two. [18]But the one who received a single talent went and dug a hole in the ground, and hid his master's money.

[19]'After a long time, the master of those slaves came back and settled accounts with them. [20]The man who had received five talents came forward and gave him the other five talents. "Master," he said, "you gave me five talents. Look: I've made another five!" [21]"Well done indeed," said his master. "You're an excellent slave, and loyal too! You've been trustworthy with small things, and now I'm going to put you in charge of bigger ones. Come and join your master's celebration!"

[22]'Then the man who had had the two talents came forward. "Master," he said, "you gave me two talents. Look: I've made another two!" [23]"Well done indeed," said his master. "You're an excellent slave, and loyal too! You've been trustworthy with small things, and now I'm going to put

you in charge of bigger ones. Come and join your master's celebration!"

[24]"Then the man who had had the one talent came forward. "Master," he said, "I knew that you were a hard man. You reap where you didn't sow, and you profit from things you never invested in. [25]So I was scared! I went and hid your talent in the ground. Here it is: it's yours, you can have it back."

[26]"'You're a wicked and lazy slave!' answered his master. "So! You knew that I reap where I didn't sow, and profit from investments I never made? [27]Then you should have put my money with the bankers, and when I got back I would have received back what I had with interest!

[28]"'So take the talent from him,' he went on, 'and give it to the man who has ten talents.' [29](If someone already has something, you see, they will be given more, and they'll have plenty. But if someone has nothing, even what they have will be taken away from them.) [30]"But as for this useless slave, throw him outside in the dark, where people weep and grind their teeth.'"

Another story about a master going away and coming back to see how the staff have been doing in his absence. Just as Jesus seems to have told several parables about farmers sowing seed (as in chapter 13), so here again, and even more in Luke's gospel, we have a further twist on a now familiar theme. But how would Jesus' first hearers have understood it?

For Jesus' first hearers, a story about a master and his servants, and about the servants being given responsibilities in the master's absence, would without a doubt have been understood in terms of God and Israel. God was the master, Israel the servant; and God had left Israel with responsibilities, with tasks to perform. This takes us right back to the Sermon on the Mount, where Jesus picked up some of the great prophetic themes of the Old Testament and declared 'you are the light of the world . . . the salt of the earth'. God had called Israel to be the means of carrying forward his great project to rescue and renew the whole creation. God had given Israel the means to do this: the Land, the Temple, the Law, the great structure of family life. Sooner or later, according to the prophets, God would return to see what his people had been doing with these gifts.

Jesus' charge against his contemporaries, repeated in one form or another throughout the gospels, was that they had failed in this God-given responsibility. They were like the third servant in the story, who, given the chance to shine, buried the talent in the ground. The result, as with the wicked tenants in chapter 21, the ungrateful guests in chapter 22 and the wicked slave in chapter 24, is that those who fail in their calling are writing themselves out of the picture. Privileges and vocations carry responsibilities; to avoid them is to forfeit the privilege or the vocation.

That seems to me to be the main, original thrust of this parable. But, to be sure, we can read it, and the church has read it for many years, in a secondary sense to do with Jesus' own calling of his followers, his gift to each of us which is to be used for his service. John Henry Newman, the great nineteenth-century writer and eventually cardinal, used to say that each of us has been put here with a particular purpose and calling which only we can do. Our task is to find out what that is and to do it. That remains true whether the purpose is playing the trumpet, cooking meals, planting trees, performing heart transplants or even preaching sermons. Sometimes, of course, it's a struggle to discover what our calling is.

Sometimes people are quite clear about their particular gifts but have no opportunity to exercise them. But each of us is called to exercise the primary, underlying gifts of living as a wise, loving human being, celebrating God's love, forgiving, praying, seeking justice, acting prudently and courageously, waiting patiently for God's will to be done. If we are trustworthy with these gifts at least, God will be ready with his answer: Well done, good and trustworthy servant. To hear those words

101

from an earthly master would bring a glow of satisfaction. To hear them from the Lord of love will be greater than the greatest delight we can imagine.

Today

Lord of all gifts, help us to use to your glory the things you have entrusted to us.

WEEK 5: THURSDAY

Matthew 25; focused on 25.31–46

[31]'When the son of man comes in his glory,' Jesus went on, 'and all the angels with him, then he will sit on his glorious throne. [32]All the nations will be assembled in front of him, and he will separate them from one another, like a shepherd separates the sheep from the goats. [33]He will stand the sheep at his right hand, and the goats at his left.

[34]'Then the king will say to those on his right, "Come here, you people who my father has blessed. Inherit the kingdom prepared for you from the foundation of the world! [35]Why? Because I was hungry and you gave me something to eat. I was thirsty and you gave me something to drink. I was a stranger and you made me welcome. [36]I was naked and you clothed me; I was sick and you looked after me; I was in prison and you came to me."

[37]'Then the righteous will answer him, "Master, when did we see you hungry and feed you, or thirsty and give you a drink? [38]When did we see you a stranger and welcome you, or naked and clothe you? [39]When did we see you sick or in prison and come to see you?"

[40]'Then the king will answer them, "I'm telling you the truth: when you did it to one of the least significant of my brothers and sisters here, you did it to me."

[41]'Then he will say to those on his left hand, "Get away from me! You're accursed! Go to the everlasting fire prepared for the devil and his angels! [42]Why? Because I was hungry and you

gave me nothing to eat! I was thirsty and you gave me nothing to drink! [43]I was a stranger and you didn't welcome me; I was naked and you didn't clothe me; I was sick and in prison and you didn't look after me!"

[44]"Then they too will answer, "Master, when did we see you hungry or thirsty, or a stranger, or naked, or sick, or in prison, and didn't do anything for you?"

[45]"Then he will answer them, "I'm telling you the truth: when you didn't do it for one of the least significant of my brothers and sisters here, you didn't do it to me."

[46]"And they will go away into everlasting punishment, but the righteous will go into everlasting life.'

One of the greatest soldiers of modern times recently published an autobiography. In it, he skates very lightly over one or two incidents in which, according to those who knew him at the time, he acted with almost incredible bravery in the face of extreme danger. But you wouldn't know that from the book.

It isn't just modesty. His memory of the incidents, he will insist, is that he was concentrating totally on the safety of the soldiers under his command. He was completely focused on doing whatever was necessary to look after them while completing the dangerous tasks he and they had been assigned.

That sense of not knowing what it was one was doing right – or, indeed, wrong – is one of the most striking elements in this remarkable tableau. (It isn't a 'parable', by the way, despite what many people say; the image of 'the sheep and the goats' in verses 32 and 33 is just an illustration, a simile, not part of a longer story about shepherds and livestock.) The theme seems to be that Jesus is offering a panoramic view of the kind of world he longed to see, the kind which would bring glory to God and which he himself would therefore approve and applaud.

We would miss the point entirely if we were to read it as a list of 'rules to be obeyed'. To be sure, if you are starting out on the path of Christian discipleship, then these are guidelines that demand close attention. But Jesus doesn't envisage us keeping a list of these actions and carefully ticking them off as we do them. He wants us to be the sort of people who do these things, as we say, 'naturally' – though actually it will be a kind of 'second nature' – without stopping to think about them.

This, of course, demands effort, particularly in the early stages. But it's an effort which springs, and has always sprung right through the course of Christian history, from people knowing Jesus, worshipping him, hearing his word and feasting at his table. Though of course people of many traditions and beliefs are kind to outcasts, visit prisoners, feed the hungry, and so on, it is noticeable, especially in our increasingly selfish society, that those who sign up for these activities on a regular basis, and who do similar things automatically even when 'off duty', are people who day by day say their prayers and week by week worship the God we know in Jesus.

That was how Christian faith spread even when the Roman emperors were determined to stamp it out. People saw the Christians behaving like this and wanted to know why. The world was full, alas, of people who didn't help, didn't feed the hungry, and didn't care for the weak and vulnerable. The Christians were modelling a new way of being human. It was, and remains, compelling.

This tableau thus stands, at the end of the last long discourse in Matthew's gospel, as the final statement of something which has been there all through. The houses on the rock and on the sand, in Matthew 7; the wheat and the tares, the good fish and the bad, in Matthew 13; and now the sheep and the goats. Matthew has highlighted the fact that Jesus intended his followers to be utterly different, people who reflected God and his love in a whole new way into the world. That is what will ultimately count. There will be surprises all round when the things people have done without thinking about them turn out to reveal their deepest characters. But there will be no doubt which of the two ways of being human is the genuine article.

Today

Gracious Lord, as we look to your future, fill us with your love, so that we may gladly serve you by serving those around us in deepest need.

WEEK 5: FRIDAY

Matthew 26.1–13

[1]So this is how it finally happened.

When Jesus had finished all these sayings, he said to his disciples, [2]'In two days' time, as you know, it'll be Passover! That's when the son of man will be handed over to be crucified.'

[3]Then the chief priests got together with the elders of the people, in the official residence of the high priest, who was called Caiaphas. [4]They plotted how to capture Jesus by some trick, and kill him.

[5]'We'd better not try anything at the feast,' they said. 'We don't want the people to riot.'

[6]While Jesus was at Bethany, in the house of Simon the leper, [7]a woman came to him who had an alabaster vase of extremely valuable ointment. She poured it on his head as he was reclining at the table.

[8]When the disciples saw it, they were furious.

'What's the point of all this waste?' they said. [9]'This could have been sold for a fortune, and the money could have been given to the poor!'

[10]Jesus knew what they were thinking.

'Why make life difficult for the woman?' he said. 'It's a lovely thing, what she's done for me. [11]You always have the poor with you, don't you? But you won't always have me. [12]When she poured this ointment on my body, you see, she did it to prepare me for my burial. [13]I'm telling you the truth: wherever this gospel is announced in all the world, what she has just done will be told, and people will remember her.'

Time to become a fly on the wall again, this time in a little house just two or three miles east of Jerusalem. If you're in the old city of Jerusalem first thing in the morning, the chances are that when the sun rises it will come up right through Bethany, the village in question.

The word 'Bethany' means, most likely, 'house of the poor'. There is some evidence that it was a place where some of the poorest people could be cared for. And it was a place where Jesus had close friends, Mary, Martha and their brother Lazarus. On this occasion, though, he was in a different house, that of 'Simon the leper' – presumably a cured leper, or he wouldn't be living in the village at all. Let's join the gathering and see what happens.

Everyone is excited because it's Passover time. After what Jesus did in Jerusalem the other day, they're all wondering what's coming next. Is he going to make another move? Is he going to give the signal for a serious uprising? He has secret contacts all over the place; are they getting swords and clubs ready for action?

The meal that evening is in full swing, when suddenly one of the women comes in. Normally women didn't join the men; it wasn't the done thing. So that's a shock for a start. But then – you shrink back in embarrassment – she's bringing a jar full of ointment, and she begins to pour it out, all over Jesus' head! You smell the delicious aroma, above the various smells of the meal, and you watch the mixture of delight and dismay on everyone's faces. What a wonderful smell; but what on earth is she up to?

Then some of Jesus' followers, perhaps expressing complex social discomfort as much as real concern, start complaining. You can see their point. Here we are in a place set aside to look after the poor, and you go pouring out a month's wages just like that? What can you be thinking about?

There is a pause. The woman looks down, ashamed at being told off and yet still pleased to have done what she did. Everyone waits. There's only one person who can settle this.

Jesus speaks. 'What's your problem?' he asks. 'This was a good thing she's done. As for the poor, there will be plenty of time to look after them; but you haven't got long to look after me. You know what she's done? She has prepared my body for burial!'

A horrified gasp goes round the room, but Jesus goes on:

'Let me tell you this! Wherever the good news is announced, right around the world, what she has done will be told. That will be her memorial.'

Now the emotions are truly mixed. The woman is both thrilled at Jesus' affirmation and distraught at the mention of burial. People look this way and that. Does he actually mean it? I know he's been talking about the Son of Man being crucified, but we all assume – or we hope – that that's just a way of talking about a time of great struggle and suffering. If he *is* actually going to die, what good news will there be to tell around the world? How does that make any sense?

Jesus may or may not have known, but he will certainly have guessed, that after his actions in the Temple the chief priests would be looking for a chance to kill him. What none of the disciples yet realized is that, for Jesus, this was not only the direct and foreseeable result of his whole kingdom-mission. It was the means by which that mission would be accomplished.

You are left in a corner of the room with one or two friends, puzzling it over, wondering what to do next. Pause there awhile and listen to what the others are saying. Then imagine that Jesus himself comes over, pulls up a chair, and starts to talk a bit more, to you in particular. What's he going to say?

Today

Lord Jesus, give us wisdom to understand your strange vocation, and to tell your good news throughout the world.

WEEK 5: SATURDAY

Matthew 26.14—27.66

[14]'Then one of the Twelve, called Judas Iscariot, went to the chief priests.

[15]'What will you give me', he said, 'to hand him over to you?'

They agreed on thirty pieces of silver. [16]From that moment on, he was watching for an opportunity to hand him over.

[17]On the first day of the Feast of Unleavened Bread, the disciples said to Jesus, 'Where do you want us to get the Passover ready for you to eat it?'

[18]'Go into the city', he said, 'to a certain man, and say to him, "The Teacher says, 'My time is very close. I'm going to keep the Passover at your house with my disciples.'"'

[19]So the disciples did as Jesus had told them, and got the Passover ready.

[20]When evening came, he settled down with the Twelve. [21]As they were eating, he said, 'I'm telling you the truth: one of you will betray me.' [22]They were extremely upset, and began to say one by one, 'It's not me, is it, Master?'

[23]'It's one who's dipped his hand with me in the dish,' Jesus replied. 'That's the one who will betray me. [24]The son of man is on his way, as the Bible said it would happen, but it's misery for the man who hands him over. It would be better for that man if he'd never been born.'

[25]At this, Judas, who was planning to betray him, said, 'It isn't me, is it, Teacher?'

'You've just said so,' he replied.

[26]As they were eating, Jesus took some bread, blessed it, broke it and gave it to the disciples.

'Take it and eat it,' he said, 'this is my body.'

[27]Then he took a cup; and, after giving thanks, he gave it to them.

'Drink this, all of you,' he said. [28]'This is my blood of the covenant, which is poured out for many for the forgiveness of sins. [29]But let me tell you this: I will not drink any more from this fruit of the vine, until that day when I drink it new with you in the kingdom of my father.'

[30]They sang a hymn, and went out to the Mount of Olives.

[31]Then Jesus said to them, 'You are all going to stumble and fall tonight because of me. This is what the Bible says, you see:

I shall strike the shepherd,
And the sheep of the flock will be scattered.

[32]'But after I am raised up, I shall go on ahead of you to Galilee.'

[33]'Even if everyone else trips and falls,' said Peter in reply to him, 'I'm never going to do that!'

[34]'I'm telling you the truth,' said Jesus to him, 'this very night, before the cock has crowed, you will deny me three times.'

[35]'Even if I have to die with you,' said Peter to him, 'I won't ever deny you!'

And all the disciples said the same.

[36]So Jesus went with them to the place called Gethsemane.

'You sit here,' he said to the disciples, 'while I go over there and pray.'

[37]He took Peter and the two sons of Zebedee with him, and began to be very upset and distressed.

[38]'My soul is overwhelmed with grief,' he said, 'even to death. Stay here and keep watch with me.'

[39]Then, going a little further on, he fell on his face and prayed.

'My father,' he said, 'if it's possible – please, please let this cup go away from me! But ... not what I want, but what you want.'

[40]He came back to the disciples and found them asleep.

'So,' he said to Peter, 'couldn't you keep watch with me for a single hour? [41]Watch and pray so that you don't get pulled down into the time of testing. The spirit is eager, but the body is weak.'

[42]Again, for the second time, he went off and said, 'My father, if it's not possible for this to pass unless I drink it, let your will be done.'

[43]Again he came and found them asleep; their eyes were heavy. [44]Once more he left them and went away. He prayed for the third time, using the same words once again. [45]Then he came back to the disciples.

'You can sleep now,' he said, 'and have a good rest! Look – the time has come, and the son of man is given over into the hands of wicked people! [46]Get up and let's be going. Look! Here comes the one who's going to betray me!'

[47]While Jesus was still speaking, there was Judas, one of the Twelve! He had come with a large crowd, with swords and clubs, from the chief priests and the elders of the people. [48]The one who was intending to betray him gave them a sign: 'The one I kiss – that's him! Grab hold of him!'

[49]So he went up at once to Jesus and said 'Greetings, Teacher!', and kissed him.

[50]'My friend,' said Jesus, 'what are you doing here?'

Then they came and laid hands on Jesus, and arrested him.

[51]At that, one of the men with Jesus reached out his hand, drew his sword and hit the high priest's slave, cutting off his ear.

[52]'Put your sword back where it belongs!' said Jesus to him. 'People who use the sword die by the sword! [53]Don't you realize that I could call on my father and have him send me more than twelve legions of angels, just like that? [54]But how then can the Bible come true when it says this has to happen?'

[55]At that time Jesus said to the crowds, 'Have you really come out with swords and sticks to arrest me, as if I were some kind of brigand? I sat there teaching in the Temple every day, and you didn't arrest me! [56]But all this has happened so that what the prophets said in the Bible would be fulfilled.'

Then all the disciples abandoned him and ran away.

⁵⁷The people who had arrested Jesus took him off to Caiaphas the high priest. The scribes and elders had already gathered at his house. ⁵⁸Peter, however, followed him at some distance, all the way to the high priest's residence. He went in and sat with the servants, to see how things would work out.

⁵⁹The high priest and the whole Council tried to produce false evidence against Jesus, to frame a capital charge and have him killed. ⁶⁰But even though they brought in plenty of lying witnesses, they couldn't find the evidence they wanted. Finally two people came forward ⁶¹and declared:

'This fellow said, "I can destroy God's Temple and build it again in three days!"'

⁶²Then the high priest stood up.

'Aren't you going to answer?' he said to him. 'What are these people accusing you of?'

⁶³But Jesus remained silent.

Then the high priest said to him,

'I put you on oath before the living God: tell us if you are the Messiah, God's son!'

⁶⁴'You said the words,' replied Jesus. 'But let me tell you this: from now on you will see "the son of man sitting at the right hand of Power, and coming on the clouds of heaven".'

⁶⁵Then the high priest tore his robes.

'He's blasphemed!' he said. 'Why do we need any more witnesses? Look – you've heard his blasphemy, here and now! ⁶⁶What's your verdict?'

'He deserves to die,' they answered.

⁶⁷Then they spat in his face and hit him. Some of them slapped him, ⁶⁸and said, 'Prophesy for us, Mr Messiah! Who was it who hit you?'

⁶⁹Meanwhile, Peter sat outside in the courtyard.

One of the servant-girls came up to him. 'You were with Jesus the Galilean too, weren't you?' she said.

⁷⁰He denied it in front of everyone.

'I don't know what you're talking about,' he said.

⁷¹He went out to the gateway. Another girl saw him, and said to the people who were there, 'This fellow was with Jesus the Nazarene!'

[72]Once more he denied it, this time swearing, 'I don't know the man!'

[73]After a little while the people standing around came up and said to Peter, 'You really are one of them! Look – the way you talk makes it obvious!'

[74]Then he began to curse and swear, 'I don't know the man!' And then, all at once, the cock crowed.

[75]And Peter remembered.

He remembered the words Jesus had spoken to him: 'Before the cock crows, you will deny me three times.'

And he went outside and cried like a baby.

27 [1]When dawn broke, all the chief priests and elders of the people held a council meeting about Jesus, in order to have him put to death. [2]They tied him up, took him off, and handed him over to Pilate, the governor.

[3]Meanwhile Judas, who had betrayed him, saw that he had been condemned, and was filled with remorse. He took the thirty pieces of silver back to the high priests and elders.

[4]'I've sinned!' he said. 'I betrayed an innocent man, and now I've got his blood on my hands!'

'See if we care!' they replied. 'It's your problem.'

[5]And he threw down the money in the Temple, and left, and went and hanged himself.

[6]'Well now,' said the chief priests, picking up the money. 'According to the law, we can't put it into the Temple treasury, because it's got blood on it.'

[7]So they had a discussion, and used it to buy the Potter's Field, as a burial place for foreigners. [8](That's why that field is called Blood Field, to this day.) [9]Then the word that was spoken by Jeremiah the prophet came true:

They took the thirty pieces of silver,
the price of the one who was valued,
valued by the children of Israel;
[10]and they gave them for the potter's field,
as the Lord instructed me.

112

[11]So Jesus stood in front of the governor.

'Are you the King of the Jews?' the governor asked him.

'If you say so,' replied Jesus.

[12]The chief priests and elders poured out their accusations against him, but he made no answer.

[13]Then Pilate said to him, 'Don't you hear all this evidence they're bringing against you?'

[14]He gave him no answer, not even a word, which quite astonished the governor.

[15]Now the governor had a custom. At festival-time he used to release one prisoner for the crowd, whoever they chose. [16]Just then they had a famous prisoner, called Jesus Barabbas. [17]So when the people were all gathered there, Pilate said to them,

'Who do you want me to release for you? Jesus Barabbas, or Jesus the so-called Messiah?' [18](He knew that they'd handed him over out of sheer envy.)

[19]While he was presiding in the court, his wife sent a message to him.

'Don't have anything to do with that man,' she said. 'He's innocent! I've had a really bad time today in a dream, all because of him.'

[20]The high priests and the elders persuaded the crowds to ask for Barabbas, and to have Jesus killed. [21]So when the governor came back to them again, and asked, 'Which of the two do you want me to release for you?' they said, 'Barabbas!'

[22]'So what shall I do with Jesus the so-called Messiah?' asked Pilate.

'Let him be crucified!' they all said.

[23]'Why?' asked Pilate. 'What's he done wrong?'

But they shouted all the louder, 'Let him be crucified!'

[24]Pilate saw that it was no good. In fact, there was a riot brewing. So he took some water and washed his hands in front of the crowd.

'I'm not guilty of this man's blood,' he said. 'It's your problem.'

[25]'Let his blood be on us!' answered all the people, 'and on our children!'

[26]Then Pilate released Barabbas for them. He had Jesus flogged, and handed him over to be crucified.

[27]Then the soldiers of the governor took Jesus into the barracks, and gathered the whole regiment together. [28]They took off his clothes and dressed him up in a scarlet military cloak. [29]They wove a crown out of thorns and stuck it on his head, and put a reed in his right hand. Then they knelt down in front of him.

'Greetings, King of the Jews!' they said, making fun of him.

[30]They spat on him. Then they took the reed and beat him about the head. [31]When they had finished mocking him, they took off the cloak, dressed him in his own clothes again, and led him off to crucify him.

[32]As they were going out they found a man from Cyrene, called Simon. They forced him to carry his cross.

[33]When they came to the place called Golgotha, which means Skull-Place, [34]they gave him a drink of wine mixed with bitter herbs. When he tasted it, he refused to drink it.

[35]So they crucified him. They divided up his clothes by casting lots, [36]and they sat down and kept watch over him there. [37]And they placed the written charge above his head: 'This is Jesus, the King of the Jews.'

[38]Then they crucified two brigands alongside him, one on his right and one on his left. [39]The people who were going by shouted blasphemies at Jesus. They shook their heads at him.

[40]'So!' they said. 'You were going to destroy the Temple and build it in three days, were you? Save yourself, if you're God's son! Come down from the cross!'

[41]The chief priests, too, and the scribes and the elders, mocked him.

[42]'He rescued others,' they said, 'but he can't rescue himself! All right, so he's the King of Israel! – well, let him come down from the cross right now, and then we'll really believe that he is! [43]He trusted in God; let God deliver him now, if he's that keen on him – after all, he did say he was God's son!'

114

⁴⁴The brigands who were crucified alongside him heaped insults on him as well.

⁴⁵From noon until mid-afternoon there was darkness over the whole land. ⁴⁶About the middle of the afternoon Jesus shouted out in a loud voice,

'Eli, Eli, lema sabachthani!'

– which means, 'My God, my God, what did you abandon me for?'

⁴⁷Some of the people who were standing there heard it and said, 'This fellow's calling Elijah!'

⁴⁸One of them ran at once and got a sponge. He filled it with vinegar, put it on a reed, and gave him a drink.

⁴⁹The others said, 'Wait a bit. Let's see if Elijah is going to come and rescue him!'

⁵⁰But Jesus shouted out loudly one more time, and then breathed his last breath.

⁵¹At that instant the Temple curtain was torn in two, from top to bottom. The earth shook, the rocks were split, ⁵²and the tombs burst open. Many bodies of the sleeping holy ones were raised. ⁵³They came out of the tombs after Jesus' resurrection, and went into the holy city, where they appeared to several people.

⁵⁴When the centurion and the others with him, keeping watch over Jesus, saw the earthquake and the things that happened, they were scared out of their wits.

'He really was God's son!' they said.

⁵⁵Several women were there, watching from a distance. They had followed Jesus from Galilee, and had given him assistance. ⁵⁶They included Mary Magdalene, Mary the mother of James and Joseph, and the mother of Zebedee's sons.

⁵⁷When evening came, a rich man from Arimathea arrived. He was called Joseph, and he, too, was a disciple of Jesus. ⁵⁸He went to Pilate and requested the body of Jesus. Pilate gave the order that it should be given to him.

⁵⁹So Joseph took the body and wrapped it in a clean linen cloth. ⁶⁰He laid it in his own new tomb, which he had carved out of the rock. Then he rolled a large stone across the doorway of the tomb, and went away.

⁶¹Mary Magdalene was there, and so was the other Mary. They were sitting opposite the tomb.

⁶²On the next day (that is, the day after Preparation Day), the chief priests and the Pharisees went as a group to Pilate.

⁶³'Sir,' they said, 'when that deceiver was still alive, we recall that he said, "After three days, I'll rise again." ⁶⁴So please give the order for the tomb to be made secure until the third day. Otherwise his disciples might come and steal him away, and then tell the people, "He's been raised from the dead!", and so the last deception would be worse than the first.'

⁶⁵'You may have a guard,' said Pilate; 'make it as secure as you know how.' ⁶⁶So they went and made the tomb secure, sealing the stone and putting a guard on watch.

It isn't me, is it?

The great story, well known yet little known, bursts upon us in a deeply disturbing scene: friends at the table discovering that one of them is to be a traitor. We often wonder what it was that made Judas do it. Perhaps we should also ask what it was that held the others back. They, like Judas, had misunderstood so much. They still didn't realize what it was Jesus had to do. There is a worried humility about their question which we would do well to imitate as we approach the narrative of Jesus' last moments, such a horribly public scene of torture and death and yet such an intimate portrait of him and those closest to him. To read this story casually, glancing through and reminding ourselves of its main outline, is to trivialize and so to misread it, like hearing a great piece of music played at ten times the proper speed. Read it with the question in mind, 'Lord, it isn't me, is it?' and see what answer you get.

Because it *is* me – and you, and all of us. We are all here somewhere. We have all been loyal and yet disloyal. We have all wanted to do the right thing and then run away when the going got tough. We have all colluded with injustice, stayed silent when we should have spoken out, and then perhaps blurted out some give-away remark when we should have shut up. And we have all stood by scenes of sorrow and tragedy, not knowing what to say or do but feeling that somehow, if only, we could or should have prevented it.

And, maybe, some or even many of us have, in time past, looked at Jesus and decided he was mad, crazy, a deluded fanatic. 'You who would destroy the temple and build it in three days, save yourself! If you are the Son of God, come down from the cross!' Many have hurled insults at Jesus; the worst, perhaps, is to patronize him by saying what a fine moral teacher he was, as though he was simply trying to be another Socrates and unfortunately got mixed up in local Jewish politics and religion. 'Lord, is it me?' If it is, or has been, then stay with that memory for a bit. Find yourself in the story, wherever you are.

Only then, perhaps, can we ask the question in a different way. Because from the earliest days of the church's life the followers of Jesus told this story for another reason. The story of Jesus became their story, in the sense that they believed *they* had died with Jesus; they had suffered with him, been crucified with him, been buried with him. Somehow – and this mystery lies at the very heart of authentic Christian experience – they believed, and knew it to be true because of the utter difference it made to life, that through baptism and faith they were living in Jesus, and he was living in them. 'Lord – is it me? Is it me, facing misunderstanding and betrayal? Is it me, praying in agony, being arrested, tried and unjustly condemned, abandoned by my friends, mocked, beaten up, stripped and hung up to die in shame?' As we read this story in faith, we should hear the answer, life-transforming as it is: 'Yes, it is you. This is who you now are. You are not the person you once were. You are the person to whom all this has happened. This is how your life is now to be shaped and directed. You are in me, and I am in you. You have died; your life is hidden, with me, in the life of God himself.'

117

All this, of course, is straight out of St Paul (another much misunderstood man). When he speaks of being 'in Christ', this is basically what he means. Jesus, the Messiah, died on the cross; you are 'in him', part of his family; therefore you died with him, were nailed to the cross with him, were buried with him. This is who you now are.

Yes, there is more. Easter and all that follows gives a further dimension. But take one thing at a time. It is through Jesus' crucifixion, Matthew insists, that he becomes what he was born to be: the saviour (1.21). And this is how he does it: by extending his arms on the cross, enfolding us in that God-with-us embrace, and bringing us with him through death into a whole new life.

Today

Thank you, loving Lord. Thank you.

HOLY WEEK: PALM SUNDAY
Psalm 31.9–16

⁹Be gracious to me, O LORD, for I am in distress;
   my eye wastes away from grief, my soul and body also.
¹⁰For my life is spent with sorrow, and my years with sighing;
   my strength fails because of my misery,
   and my bones waste away.
¹¹I am the scorn of all my adversaries,
   a horror to my neighbours,
   an object of dread to my acquaintances;
   those who see me in the street flee from me.
¹²I have passed out of mind like one who is dead;
   I have become like a broken vessel.
¹³For I hear the whispering of many – terror all around! –
   as they scheme together against me,
   as they plot to take my life.
¹⁴But I trust in you, O LORD;
   I say, 'You are my God.'

¹⁵My times are in your hand;
    deliver me from the hand of my enemies and persecutors.
¹⁶Let your face shine upon your servant;
    save me in your steadfast love.

I have on my shelves a Bible that my grandfather used when he was a student, a hundred or so years ago. It's good to have that sort of contact with earlier generations, but what pleases me particularly is being able to see how he read it, what was important to him in it. Here are his underlinings of particular passages. Here are the things he scribbled in the margins. When I remember him from my boyhood, he comes across as a cheerful, outdoor, friendly man. All that was true. But here, in his private jottings, I trace something of the inner man, and how he became who he was.

That is a small window on what we ought to think and feel as we read the Psalms and think of Jesus. It's passages like this that make it obvious; but really we should sense, all through the Psalter, his quiet presence, inhabiting the ancient traditions of his people, pondering and praying through the joys and the sorrows, reflecting on the portrait of the coming king, agonizing over the constant refrain of sorrow and exile. Here, if we listen carefully, we trace something of how Jesus became who he was. 'Even though he was the Son,' says an early Christian writer, 'he learned obedience by what he suffered' (Hebrews 5.8). And, as we read the Psalms, we realize how he learned that obedience. His own praying had been formed by these poems. We are privileged to pray them with him, sensing his presence as we do so.

It would be good to read the whole Psalm, of course, not just these central eight verses. According to Luke (23.46), Jesus prayed verse 5 ('into your hand I commit my spirit') as he hung dying on the cross. The opening of the Psalm sets the agony of the central passage into the context of a rock-bottom trust in God, despite all that the world can do. The closing passage, too, celebrates God's continuing and abundant goodness and protection. But here, in the middle, we find the passage which meant that, when Jesus was plotted against, whispered about, picked up by the soldiers, laughed at, spat at, abandoned by his friends, he knew this didn't mean he had somehow fallen out of God's hands. It didn't mean he had taken a wrong turn.

This lesson is vital for the church as a whole and for every individual Christian. Of course, it is possible to take a wrong turn and suffer the consequences. It's no use quoting these verses if you have rebelled and gone your own way, and find yourself in a mess as a result. The right thing then is to repent and get back on course as quickly as possible. But if, so far as you know, you have faithfully trusted and followed, and then find yourself in this kind of distress, lonely and misunderstood, it may be that this is simply part of your particular call to join in the prayer of Jesus, the suffering of Jesus, so that his life and joy may also be revealed in you and through you. Read 2 Corinthians 4 and see how one very early Christian came to exactly this conclusion, using the Psalms to help him.

And when the church as a whole finds itself in difficulties – lack of money, mocked in the media, perplexed about what to do next – that doesn't necessarily mean it's taken a wrong turn, either. Of course, scandals and divisions are shameful. It is all too possible for the church to get it horribly wrong. When that happens it must say sorry, to God and to everyone who's been affected. But sometimes God's people as a whole are called to follow their Lord through the darkness as well as into the light. That's why the Psalms remain indispensable in our public worship as well as our private prayer.

Today

Thank you, gracious Lord, that we can share your own prayer as we go through the darkness. Help us this coming week to stay close to you and to share your faith and hope.

HOLY WEEK: MONDAY
Matthew 26.14–35

[14]Then one of the Twelve, called Judas Iscariot, went to the chief priests.

[15]'What will you give me', he said, 'to hand him over to you?'

They agreed on thirty pieces of silver. [16]From that moment on, he was watching for an opportunity to hand him over.

[17]On the first day of the Feast of Unleavened Bread, the disciples said to Jesus, 'Where do you want us to get the Passover ready for you to eat it?'

[18]'Go into the city', he said, 'to a certain man, and say to him, "The Teacher says, 'My time is very close. I'm going to keep the Passover at your house with my disciples.'"'

[19]So the disciples did as Jesus had told them, and got the Passover ready.

[20]When evening came, he settled down with the Twelve. [21]As they were eating, he said, 'I'm telling you the truth: one of you will betray me.' [22]They were extremely upset, and began to say one by one, 'It's not me, is it, Master?'

[23]'It's one who's dipped his hand with me in the dish,' Jesus replied. 'That's the one who will betray me. [24]The son of man is on his way, as the Bible said it would happen, but it's misery for the man who hands him over. It would be better for that man if he'd never been born.'

[25]At this, Judas, who was planning to betray him, said, 'It isn't me, is it, Teacher?'

'You've just said so,' he replied.

[26]As they were eating, Jesus took some bread, blessed it, broke it and gave it to the disciples.

'Take it and eat it,' he said, 'this is my body.'

[27]Then he took a cup; and, after giving thanks, he gave it to them.

'Drink this, all of you,' he said. [28]'This is my blood of the covenant, which is poured out for many for the forgiveness of sins. [29]But let me tell you this: I will not drink any more from this fruit of the vine, until that day when I drink it new with you in the kingdom of my father.'

[30]They sang a hymn, and went out to the Mount of Olives.

[31]Then Jesus said to them, 'You are all going to stumble and fall tonight because of me. This is what the Bible says, you see:

I shall strike the shepherd,
And the sheep of the flock will be scattered.

[32]'But after I am raised up, I shall go on ahead of you to Galilee.'

[33]'Even if everyone else trips and falls,' said Peter in reply to him, 'I'm never going to do that!'

[34]'I'm telling you the truth,' said Jesus to him, 'this very night, before the cock has crowed, you will deny me three times.'

[35]'Even if I have to die with you,' said Peter to him, 'I won't ever deny you!'

And all the disciples said the same.

Some of the sharpest, most bitter arguments the church has ever had have been about the meaning of the meal which Jesus shared with his friends the night before he died, and of the similar meals his friends have shared ever since. In the sixteenth century, in particular, these arguments exploded in several directions as Christians accused one another of perverting or even undermining altogether the point and purpose of this meal.

That is tragic, of course, but the present passage indicates that we should not after all be surprised. The story of Jesus sharing the bread and the wine, in those four brief verses 26–29, is surrounded by the discussion of the betrayal that was about to happen (verses 14–16, 20–25) and the warning that all the disciples would abandon him, and that Peter, particularly, would deny him (verses 30–35). Perhaps it is always so.

Perhaps, whenever something truly and massively important is afoot, it becomes the place where attack is concentrated, where Jesus' friends will be distracted by so many immediate muddles and concerns that they risk missing the glorious thing that stands quietly in the centre, the gleaming diamond in the middle of the rubbish-heap.

And diamond it is – with many facets, reflecting light all around. This meal, this Passover-with-a-difference, was the way Jesus chose to explain to his followers what his death was all about. They hadn't understood what he'd said to them up to this point, but this meal, and their repeating of it thereafter, would soak it deep down into their imaginations. What you do, and particularly what you eat and drink, changes the way you think and feel. Jesus wanted them, and us, to know at a level much deeper than mere theory that his death was the true Passover, the time when God acted to rescue his people from slavery once and for all, and that we are not merely spectators but participants and beneficiaries. When we come to the table, as Paul said to the Corinthians, we truly share in his body and blood (1 Corinthians 10.16). We are shaped and formed, together and individually, as Passover-people, as rescued-from-slavery people, as dying-with-Jesus people.

For a community to be formed and shaped in that way is perhaps the most powerful thing that can happen to a group of people. Again, that's why it's so easy to distort it, to allow squabbles and muddles and even betrayals and denials to creep in and spoil it. Sometimes the church has made its sharing of this meal into such a wonderful work of art that everyone is thinking about how clever the art is rather than about how awesome Jesus is. Other Christians have over-reacted to this, and come to the meal, when they have to, almost casually or flippantly, like someone whisking through an art gallery with a cheerful comment about the pretty paintings. We all need, constantly, to find our way back into the heart and meaning of this meal. As Jesus makes clear in verse 29, this meal is the prelude to the coming of the kingdom – which must mean that Jesus himself, and Matthew in shaping his gospel the way he has, saw his death, interpreted in this Passover-fashion, as the final act of kingdom-bringing.

Certainly that is the implication of 28.18. Jesus' death is the final overthrow of the powers of darkness, which is why his resurrection then establishes him as the one who has all authority in heaven and on earth. However puzzled we may be (if all this is anywhere near the truth, we should hardly expect to understand such a huge and mysterious thing straight off), we are called to share the meal, to stay focused on Jesus as the rescuer, the kingdom-bringer, and so to encourage one another to be kingdom-people. To be Jesus-people.

Today

Help us, gracious Lord, to come to your table in gratitude and love, that we may be formed into your people and be strengthened in your service.

HOLY WEEK: TUESDAY

Matthew 26.36–56

[36]So Jesus went with them to the place called Gethsemane.

'You sit here,' he said to the disciples, 'while I go over there and pray.'

[37]He took Peter and the two sons of Zebedee with him, and began to be very upset and distressed.

[38]'My soul is overwhelmed with grief,' he said, 'even to death. Stay here and keep watch with me.'

[39]Then, going a little further on, he fell on his face and prayed.

'My father,' he said, 'if it's possible – please, please let this cup go away from me! But . . . not what I want, but what you want.'

⁴⁰He came back to the disciples and found them asleep.

'So,' he said to Peter, 'couldn't you keep watch with me for a single hour? ⁴¹Watch and pray so that you don't get pulled down into the time of testing. The spirit is eager, but the body is weak.'

⁴²Again, for the second time, he went off and said, 'My father, if it's not possible for this to pass unless I drink it, let your will be done.'

⁴³Again he came and found them asleep; their eyes were heavy. ⁴⁴Once more he left them and went away. He prayed for the third time, using the same words once again. ⁴⁵Then he came back to the disciples.

'You can sleep now,' he said, 'and have a good rest! Look – the time has come, and the son of man is given over over into the hands of wicked people! ⁴⁶Get up and let's be going. Look! Here comes the one who's going to betray me!'

⁴⁷While Jesus was still speaking, there was Judas, one of the Twelve! He had come with a large crowd, with swords and clubs, from the chief priests and the elders of the people. ⁴⁸The one who was intending to betray him gave them a sign: 'The one I kiss – that's him! Grab hold of him!'

⁴⁹So he went up at once to Jesus and said 'Greetings, Teacher!', and kissed him.

⁵⁰'My friend,' said Jesus, 'what are you doing here?'

Then they came and laid hands on Jesus, and arrested him.

⁵¹At that, one of the men with Jesus reached out his hand, drew his sword and hit the high priest's slave, cutting off his ear.

⁵²'Put your sword back where it belongs!' said Jesus to him. 'People who use the sword die by the sword! ⁵³Don't you realize that I could call on my father and have him send me more than twelve legions of angels, just like that? ⁵⁴But how then can the Bible come true when it says this has to happen?'

⁵⁵At that time Jesus said to the crowds, 'Have you really come out with swords and sticks to arrest me, as if I were some

kind of brigand? I sat there teaching in the Temple every day, and you didn't arrest me! [56]But all this has happened so that what the prophets said in the Bible would be fulfilled.'

Then all the disciples abandoned him and ran away.

Put this passage alongside the other time when Jesus took Peter, James and John away with him by themselves. In chapter 17, the four of them went up a mountain, and the disciples watched in amazement as Jesus was transfigured before them, shining with the glory of God and talking with Moses and Elijah. Now the same group of three are together in a garden, and the disciples watch in amazement as once again Jesus is transfigured, this time with the sorrow of God. Again, he is very much aware of the ancient scriptures which said it must be like this (verses 24, 54, 56).

This scene in Gethsemane is absolutely central to any proper understanding of who Jesus really was. It's all too easy for devout Christians to imagine him as a kind of demigod, striding heroically through the world without a care. Some have even read John's gospel that way, though I believe that is to misread it. But certainly Matthew is clear that at this crucial moment Jesus had urgent and agitating business to do with his father. He had come this far; he had told them, again and again, that he would be handed over, tortured and crucified; but now, at the last minute, this knowledge had to make its way down from his scripture-soaked mind into his obedient, praying heart. And it is wonderfully comforting (as the writer to the Hebrews points out) that he had to make this agonizing journey of faith, just as we do.

'If it's possible – please make it that I don't have to drink this cup!' The 'cup' in question, without a doubt, is the 'cup of God's wrath', as in many biblical passages (Isaiah 51.17; Jeremiah 25.15, and elsewhere). Jesus was resolutely determined to understand this fateful moment in the light of the long scriptural narrative that he saw now coming to its climax in his death. But, precisely because of that, he realized in a new and devastating way that he was called to go down into the darkness, deeper than anyone had gone before, the darkness of one who, though he was the very son of God, would drink the cup which symbolized God's wrath against all that is evil, all that destroys and defaces God's wonderful world and his image-bearing creatures.

We can see this very process working its way out as the story unwinds. All the strands of evil in the world seem to rush together upon him. The power-seeking politics of the local elite. The casual brutality of imperial Rome. The disloyalty of Judas. The failure of Peter. The large systems which crush those in their way, and the intimate, sharply personal, betrayals. And everything in between, the scorn, the misunderstanding, the violence. The story is told in such a way that we see and feel, rather than just think about, the many different manifestations of evil in the world. Matthew invites us to see them all converging on Jesus. That is what this story is all about.

We are encouraged to see this scene, too, as somehow a revelation of the glory of God. It is one thing to be transfigured in the sense of shining with the dazzling light of God's glory. It is another thing, perhaps equal if not greater, to be seen in agony, sharing the sorrow and pain of the world. Perhaps the two scenes need each other to be complete. Certainly our own pilgrimage, if we are faithful, will have elements of both. One of the reasons we read and reread this extraordinary story is because we know, in our deepest beings, that the scriptural story to which Jesus was obedient must be our story too. Matthew, telling us that Jesus' disciples all forsook him and fled, wants us by contrast to stay the course, to see this thing through, to witness the glory of God in the suffering face of his crucified son.

Today

Teach us, good Lord, to watch with you in your suffering, that we may learn also to see your glory.

HOLY WEEK: WEDNESDAY
Matthew 26.57–75

[57]The people who had arrested Jesus took him off to Caiaphas the high priest. The scribes and elders had already gathered at his house. [58]Peter, however, followed him at some distance, all the way to the high priest's residence. He went in and sat with the servants, to see how things would work out.

[59]The high priest and the whole Council tried to produce false evidence against Jesus, to frame a capital charge and have him killed. [60]But even though they brought in plenty of lying witnesses, they couldn't find the evidence they wanted. Finally two people came forward [61]and declared:

'This fellow said, "I can destroy God's Temple and build it again in three days!"'

[62]Then the high priest stood up.

'Aren't you going to answer?' he said to him. 'What are these people accusing you of?'

[63]But Jesus remained silent.

Then the high priest said to him,

'I put you on oath before the living God: tell us if you are the Messiah, God's son!'

[64]'You said the words,' replied Jesus. 'But let me tell you this: from now on you will see "the son of man sitting at the right hand of Power, and coming on the clouds of heaven".'

[65]Then the high priest tore his robes.

'He's blasphemed!' he said. 'Why do we need any more witnesses? Look – you've heard his blasphemy, here and now! [66]What's your verdict?'

'He deserves to die,' they answered.

[67]Then they spat in his face and hit him. Some of them slapped him, [68]and said, 'Prophesy for us, Mr Messiah! Who was it who hit you?'

[69]Meanwhile, Peter sat outside in the courtyard.

One of the servant-girls came up to him. 'You were with Jesus the Galilean too, weren't you?' she said.

[70]He denied it in front of everyone.

'I don't know what you're talking about,' he said.

[71]He went out to the gateway. Another girl saw him, and said to the people who were there, 'This fellow was with Jesus the Nazarene!'

[72]Once more he denied it, this time swearing, 'I don't know the man!'

[73]After a little while the people standing around came up and said to Peter, 'You really are one of them! Look – the way you talk makes it obvious!'

[74]Then he began to curse and swear, 'I don't know the man!' And then, all at once, the cock crowed.

[75]And Peter remembered.

He remembered the words Jesus had spoken to him: 'Before the cock crows, you will deny me three times.'

And he went outside and cried like a baby.

When I first lived in London, I already knew four or five parts of the city quite well. I knew Westminster itself, with the Abbey, the Houses of Parliament, and the roads leading up to Buckingham Palace. I knew the areas around the big cricket grounds. I knew the British Museum and Oxford Street, and one or two other places I had had to visit from time to time. But I had no idea how they joined up. I used to get about on the Underground, being whisked from place to place with no mental picture of what was above me. So if I tried to walk between the places I knew I would get quite lost.

Many people are like that with the stories in the gospels. They know the parables and the miracles. They know about Jesus' birth; about the transfiguration, perhaps; certainly about his riding into Jerusalem on a donkey, cleansing the Temple, and then his trial and death. But even with these final events they may have little or no idea how they join up. The cycle of readings in church carries them from event to event, like a spiritual Underground train, and they've never thought about how things actually moved from one thing to another in the real world.

So people often miss the full force of the questions Caiaphas asked Jesus in this informal night hearing. The chief priests were the guardians of the Temple. That was (in our terms) as much a political office as a spiritual one, and they took it extremely seriously. Jesus hadn't actually committed any crime in what he'd done in the Temple, but they were eager to make the links with his larger intentions. Word had got around, in a garbled form, that at some point he'd said something about destroying the Temple and rebuilding it. That could only mean one thing. The only person (other than the high priest) who could claim authority over the Temple was the Messiah. And, of course, God himself. So did Jesus' actions and words mean . . . ?

Before we can get there, we need to remind ourselves of another link of thought which they would have made. Some Jewish teachers pondered passages like Genesis 1.26, where God says 'Let *us* make humankind in our own image', and Daniel 7.13, where the prophet sees a vision of 'one like a son of man' coming on the clouds to the 'Ancient of Days' and being enthroned beside him. As they did so, some speculated that there might be some kind of plurality within God himself. Such ideas were severely frowned on by most people. Again, it's as much the political as the spiritual claim that was seen as dangerous, blaspheming nonsense.

So when Jesus refuses to answer the question about destroying the Temple and rebuilding it in three days, the high priest moves to the natural next step. He puts Jesus on oath, and asks him, 'Are you the Messiah, the Son of God?'

Jesus' reply is fully in line with all that we have seen in the earlier pages of Matthew's gospel. It all joins up. The high priest himself has said what needs to be said, but there is more:

Caiaphas will see that Jesus will be vindicated by God after his suffering, that he will 'come with the clouds of heaven' and be enthroned at the right hand of 'Power', in other words, of God himself.

That's enough! It's blasphemy! And Jesus is condemned, mocked as a false prophet.

Meanwhile, a different sort of connection is established out in the courtyard. Peter – impetuous, blundering Peter – provides the mirror-image to Jesus. Jesus tells the truth, knowing it will condemn him. Peter tells a lie to save his skin. The stage is set. Jesus, the innocent one, will die in place of Peter, the guilty. And the rest of us, too.

Today

Thank you, Lord Jesus, for the truth which you spoke and lived, and for which you died. Help us, afraid as we are of truth, to come out of the shadows and confess that we are your followers.

HOLY WEEK: MAUNDY THURSDAY
Matthew 27.1–32

27 ¹When dawn broke, all the chief priests and elders of the people held a council meeting about Jesus, in order to have him put to death. ²They tied him up, took him off, and handed him over to Pilate, the governor.

³Meanwhile Judas, who had betrayed him, saw that he had been condemned, and was filled with remorse. He took the thirty pieces of silver back to the high priests and elders.

⁴'I've sinned!' he said. 'I betrayed an innocent man, and now I've got his blood on my hands!'

'See if we care!' they replied. 'It's your problem.'

⁵And he threw down the money in the Temple, and left, and went and hanged himself.

⁶'Well now,' said the chief priests, picking up the money. 'According to the law, we can't put it into the Temple treasury, because it's got blood on it.'

[7]So they had a discussion, and used it to buy the Potter's Field, as a burial place for foreigners. [8](That's why that field is called Blood Field, to this day.) [9]Then the word that was spoken by Jeremiah the prophet came true:

> They took the thirty pieces of silver,
> the price of the one who was valued,
> valued by the children of Israel;
> [10]and they gave them for the potter's field,
> as the Lord instructed me.

[11]So Jesus stood in front of the governor.

'Are you the King of the Jews?' the governor asked him.

'If you say so,' replied Jesus.

[12]The chief priests and elders poured out their accusations against him, but he made no answer.

[13]Then Pilate said to him, 'Don't you hear all this evidence they're bringing against you?'

[14]He gave him no answer, not even a word, which quite astonished the governor.

[15]Now the governor had a custom. At festival-time he used to release one prisoner for the crowd, whoever they chose. [16]Just then they had a famous prisoner, called Jesus Barabbas. [17]So when the people were all gathered there, Pilate said to them,

'Who do you want me to release for you? Jesus Barabbas, or Jesus the so-called Messiah?' [18](He knew that they'd handed him over out of sheer envy.)

[19]While he was presiding in the court, his wife sent a message to him.

'Don't have anything to do with that man,' she said. 'He's innocent! I've had a really bad time today in a dream, all because of him.'

[20]The high priests and the elders persuaded the crowds to ask for Barabbas, and to have Jesus killed. [21]So when the governor came back to them again, and asked, 'Which of the two do you want me to release for you?' they said, 'Barabbas!'

²²'So what shall I do with Jesus the so-called Messiah?' asked Pilate.

'Let him be crucified!' they all said.

²³'Why?' asked Pilate. 'What's he done wrong?'

But they shouted all the louder, 'Let him be crucified!'

²⁴Pilate saw that it was no good. In fact, there was a riot brewing. So he took some water and washed his hands in front of the crowd.

'I'm not guilty of this man's blood,' he said. 'It's your problem.'

²⁵'Let his blood be on us!' answered all the people, 'and on our children!'

²⁶Then Pilate released Barabbas for them. He had Jesus flogged, and handed him over to be crucified.

²⁷Then the soldiers of the governor took Jesus into the barracks, and gathered the whole regiment together. ²⁸They took off his clothes and dressed him up in a scarlet military cloak. ²⁹They wove a crown out of thorns and stuck it on his head, and put a reed in his right hand. Then they knelt down in front of him.

'Greetings, King of the Jews!' they said, making fun of him.

³⁰They spat on him. Then they took the reed and beat him about the head. ³¹When they had finished mocking him, they took off the cloak, dressed him in his own clothes again, and led him off to crucify him.

³²As they were going out they found a man from Cyrene, called Simon. They forced him to carry his cross.

A few years ago there was a great railway disaster. Two trains, approaching London, speeded on to the same bit of track. Many were killed, several injured.

There was a long official enquiry. At the end of it, after countless hours of agonizing testimony, a report emerged. It was a grievous mistake, said the report. But there was nobody really to blame.

I have oversimplified, of course. But again and again that seems to be the verdict in such cases. Yes, it was terrible. But no, it wasn't really anybody's fault. Most of us, looking on, can't quite get our heads round that.

Matthew has told the story of the events that led up to Jesus' death in order to make exactly the opposite point. Yes, this was a terrible event. And yes, *it was everybody's fault.* The chief priests have already shown their true colours, and are clearly to blame. Now Judas realizes his own guilt. Then Pilate plays his own cynical game: some have suggested that he was a good man, trying his best to have Jesus acquitted, but most likely his main motive was to try to establish his superiority over the chief priests. Then the crowd join in, and they help the priests to beat him at his own game. But he was certainly to blame as well.

Then the soldiers join in the fun. King of the Jews, eh? We'll see about that. The previous mockery, in front of the chief priests, was making fun of Jesus' claim to be a prophet (26.67–68). This time it's the claim to be king.

The point is that they all contribute. The crowd may indeed have shouted 'his blood be on us, and on our children' (verse 25) – a chilling phrase which has been horribly abused by many so-called Christians who have used it as an excuse to persecute Jewish people, Jesus' own blood relatives. But Matthew's point is that, though the crowd are indeed complicit, everyone else is too. Only the minor characters like Pilate's wife (verse 19) and Simon of Cyrene (verse 32) stand out in the other direction, and they can do nothing to stop the brutal killing of the innocent Jesus.

We may begin by watching from the sidelines, but the story is designed to draw us in. We find ourselves there in the crowd, shouting like football supporters for this man rather than the notorious Barabbas (the first person in history, but by no means the last, to discover that Jesus was dying in his place). We feel the surge of emotion, of anger that our national hopes have been trampled on by this upstart from Galilee. Or, in the back room of Pilate's headquarters, we find the soldiers, so long fed up with having to police Jewish uprisings, finally discovering someone on whom they can take out their frustrations. These things happen, we think. This is how people react. And, in a sense, who can blame them? That's how it is.

It is precisely 'how it is' that sent Jesus to the cross. Matthew is telling us, in these vivid and shocking human scenes, what Jesus' death is all about. There is a dark twist in 'the way things are'. Jesus came to enter that darkness, to have his own body twisted in pain on the cross, so that the world could be straightened out, so that light could dawn at last.

Today

Almighty God, as the darkness closes around Jesus, help us, like Simon, to carry his cross, to be there with him to the end.

HOLY WEEK: GOOD FRIDAY

Matthew 27.33–56

[33]When they came to the place called Golgotha, which means Skull-Place, [34]they gave him a drink of wine mixed with bitter herbs. When he tasted it, he refused to drink it.

[35]So they crucified him. They divided up his clothes by casting lots, [36]and they sat down and kept watch over him there. [37]And they placed the written charge above his head: 'This is Jesus, the King of the Jews.'

[38]Then they crucified two brigands alongside him, one on his right and one on his left. [39]The people who were going by shouted blasphemies at Jesus. They shook their heads at him.

[40]'So!' they said. 'You were going to destroy the Temple and build it in three days, were you? Save yourself, if you're God's son! Come down from the cross!'

[41]The chief priests, too, and the scribes and the elders, mocked him.

[42]'He rescued others,' they said, 'but he can't rescue himself! All right, so he's the King of Israel! – well, let him come down

from the cross right now, and then we'll really believe that he is! [43]He trusted in God; let God deliver him now, if he's that keen on him – after all, he did say he was God's son!'

[44]The brigands who were crucified alongside him heaped insults on him as well.

[45]From noon until mid-afternoon there was darkness over the whole land. [46]About the middle of the afternoon Jesus shouted out in a loud voice,

'Eli, Eli, lema sabachthani!'

– which means, 'My God, my God, what did you abandon me for?'

[47]Some of the people who were standing there heard it and said, 'This fellow's calling Elijah!'

[48]One of them ran at once and got a sponge. He filled it with vinegar, put it on a reed, and gave him a drink.

[49]The others said, 'Wait a bit. Let's see if Elijah is going to come and rescue him!'

[50]But Jesus shouted out loudly one more time, and then breathed his last breath.

[51]At that instant the Temple curtain was torn in two, from top to bottom. The earth shook, the rocks were split, [52]and the tombs burst open. Many bodies of the sleeping holy ones were raised. [53]They came out of the tombs after Jesus' resurrection, and went into the holy city, where they appeared to several people.

[54]When the centurion and the others with him, keeping watch over Jesus, saw the earthquake and the things that happened, they were scared out of their wits.

'He really was God's son!' they said.

[55]Several women were there, watching from a distance. They had followed Jesus from Galilee, and had given him assistance. [56]They included Mary Magdalene, Mary the mother of James and Joseph, and the mother of Zebedee's sons.

Overwhelmed with horror at what we are seeing, we join the crowds as they hurry along behind the soldiers with their prisoner. Forget the calm tableau of so many historic paintings of the scene, with Mary and John standing at a discreet distance from the foot of Jesus' cross. In the Middle East, then as now, there were always more people in the crowd than would fit into the small streets, always people pushing and shoving. The soldiers might keep people at arm's length, but not much more. There were probably fifty people within ten feet of Jesus, jostling, shouting, jeering, pointing, spitting. Some weeping.

You could tell the story a thousand different ways, and they'd all be true. Jesus' followers quickly came to tell it in such a way as to bring out what Jesus himself had been trying to say all along, and what Matthew has been trying to tell us throughout his gospel: this is the event through which Jesus became king. King of the Jews. King of the world.

To see how Matthew has done this, you have to imagine yourself, in that crowd, as someone who has prayed and sung the Psalms all your life. The Psalms turn the hard lumps of Israel's story and hopes into liquid poetry, flowing along like a great river, carrying you with it. And as you stand at the foot of the cross, you have a nightmarish sequence of flashbacks, of déjà vu moments, watching Israel's hopes and dreams come to life, or rather to death, in front of your eyes. Bits and pieces of the Psalms, acted out right there. Jesus is offered sour wine to drink. They cast lots for his clothes. They hail him as 'king of the Jews'. They mock him with his own words. And, after three hours of darkness, Jesus screams out the words that begin the Psalm (22) where some of those things happen: 'My God, my God, why have you forsaken me?' The fulfilment has come, and it is a moment of utter terror and hopelessness. It is as though the sun were to rise one day and it would be a black sun, bringing a darkness deeper than the night itself.

As you stand there in this strange, powerful mixture of recognition and horror, bring bit by bit into the picture the stories on which you have lived. Bring the hopes you had when you were young. Bring the bright vision of family life, of success in sport or work or art, the dreams of exciting adventures in far-off places. Bring the joy of seeing a new baby, full of promise and possibility. Bring the longings of your heart. They are all fulfilled here, though not in the way you imagined. This is the way God fulfilled the dreams of his people. This is how the coming king would overcome all his enemies.

Or bring the fears and sorrows you had when you were young. The terror of violence, perhaps at home. The shame of failure at school, of rejection by friends. The nasty comments that hurt you then and hurt you still. The terrible moment when you realized a wonderful relationship had come to an end. The sudden, meaningless death of someone you loved very much. They are all fulfilled here, too. God has taken them upon himself, in the person of his Son. This is the earthquake moment, the darkness-at-noon moment, the moment of terror and sudden faith, as even the hard-boiled Roman soldier blurts out at the end. (Don't forget that 'Son of God' was a regular title claimed by Caesar, his boss.)

But then bring the hopes and sorrows of the world. Bring the millions who are homeless because of flood or famine. Bring the children orphaned by AIDS or war. Bring the politicians who begin by longing for justice and end up hoping for bribes. Bring the beautiful and fragile earth on which we live. Think of God's dreams for his creation, and God's sorrow at its ruin.

As we stand there by the cross, let the shouting and pushing and the angry faces fade away for a moment, and look at the slumped head of Jesus. The hopes and fears of all the years are met in him, here on the cross. God chose Israel to be his way of rescuing the world. God sent Jesus to be his way of rescuing Israel. Jesus went to the cross to fulfil that double mission. His cross, planted in the middle of the jostling, uncomprehending, mocking world of his day and ours, stands as the symbol of a victory unlike any other. A love unlike any other. A God unlike any other.

Today

Thank you, Lord Jesus, for all that you bore that day. Thank you for your victory, the victory of love and justice. Thank you that you are the Son of God.

HOLY WEEK: HOLY SATURDAY
Matthew 27.57–66

[57]When evening came, a rich man from Arimathea arrived. He was called Joseph, and he, too, was a disciple of Jesus. [58]He went to Pilate and requested the body of Jesus. Pilate gave the order that it should be given to him.

[59]So Joseph took the body and wrapped it in a clean linen cloth. [60]He laid it in his own new tomb, which he had carved out of the rock. Then he rolled a large stone across the doorway of the tomb, and went away.

[61]Mary Magdalene was there, and so was the other Mary. They were sitting opposite the tomb.

[62]On the next day (that is, the day after Preparation Day), the chief priests and the Pharisees went as a group to Pilate.

[63]'Sir,' they said, 'when that deceiver was still alive, we recall that he said, "After three days, I'll rise again." [64]So please give the order for the tomb to be made secure until the third day. Otherwise his disciples might come and steal him away, and then tell the people, "He's been raised from the dead!", and so the last deception would be worse than the first.'

[65]'You may have a guard,' said Pilate; 'make it as secure as you know how.' [66]So they went and made the tomb secure, sealing the stone and putting a guard on watch.

They tried to keep Jesus safely dead then, and they try it still today.

Again and again, when the newspapers or the radio stations want to talk about God, they ignore Jesus. We hear experts proclaiming that science has disproved God – without realizing that the 'god' you could squeeze out of the picture by more and more scientific discoveries is not the God whom Christians worship. Our world is still full of the modern equivalents of high priests going to the governor to have a guard placed on the tomb – the sceptics appealing for help to the powerful. It didn't work then and it won't work now.

Sometimes, though, we Christians need to observe a Holy Saturday moment. On Holy Saturday, there is nothing you can do except wait. The Christian faith suffers, apparently, great defeats. There are scandals and divisions, and the world looks on and loves it, like the crowds at the foot of the cross. When the Pope visited the United Kingdom in September 2010, he spent almost all his time talking about Jesus while the commentators in the media spent almost all their time talking about sex. And where the church, through its own fault, has caused scandal, a time of silence may be appropriate.

But God will do what God will do, in God's own time. The world can plot and plan, but all of that will count for nothing when the victory already won on the cross turns into the new sort of victory on the third day. In many parts of the western world today, the church is almost apologetic, afraid of being sneered at. It looks as though the chief priests of our culture, the Pharisees in today's media, and even the political leaders, have won. Give them their day to imagine that. It's happened before and it will happen again. The Romans tried to stamp out the Christian faith once and for all at the end of the third century, but within a few years more than half the empire had converted and the new emperor gave in. Many people in England were sceptical about Christian faith after the religious turmoil of the sixteenth and seventeenth centuries, but great revivals of various different sorts took place in the eighteenth

HOLY WEEK: HOLY SATURDAY Matthew 27.57–66

and nineteenth. Who knows what will happen next, after the sneering and scheming of the sceptics of our day? Our part is to keep Holy Saturday in faith and hope, grieving over the ruin of the world that sent Jesus to his death, trusting in the promises of God that new life will come in his way and his time.

And there is usually something to be done in the present, even when times are sad and hard. It took considerable courage for Joseph of Arimathea to go to Pontius Pilate and ask for Jesus' body. Peter and the others had run away to hide because they were afraid of being thought accomplices of Jesus. Joseph had no such qualms, even after Jesus' death.

Some of Jesus' followers might well have thought that, if the Romans had crucified him, he can't have been the Messiah, so he must have been a charlatan. They might willingly have let the Romans bury him in a common grave, as they usually did after a crucifixion (always supposing there was anything left to bury once dogs, birds and vermin had done their work). But Joseph didn't see it that way. A clean linen cloth; the tomb he had prepared for himself; and the security of a great stone.

It all had to be done in haste, with the sabbath approaching (that's why the two Marys were watching, so they could go back on the first day of the new week to complete what should be done to the body). But what was done was done decently. Sometimes, as we work for and with Jesus, it may feel a bit like that. We aren't sure why we've got to this place, why things aren't going as we wanted or planned, and the life seems to have drained out of it all. That's a Holy Saturday moment. Do what has to be done, and wait for God to act in his own way and his own time.

Today

Help us, gracious Lord, to wait for your victory, and in the meantime to serve you in whatever way we can.

EASTER DAY

Matthew 28.1–10

[1]Dawn was breaking on the first day of the week; the sabbath was over. Mary Magdalene, and the other Mary, had come to look at the tomb, [2]when suddenly there was a great earthquake. An angel of the Lord came down from heaven. He came to the stone, rolled it away, and sat down on top of it. [3]Looking at him was like looking at lightning, and his clothes were white, like snow. [4]The guards trembled with terror at him, and became like corpses themselves.

[5]'Don't be afraid,' said the angel to the women. 'I know you're looking for Jesus, who was crucified. [6]He isn't here! He's been raised, as he said he would be! Come and see the place where he was lying – [7]and then go at once, and tell his disciples that he's been raised from the dead, and that he's going on ahead of you to Galilee. That's where you'll see him. There: I've told you.'

[8]The women scurried off quickly, away from the tomb, in a mixture of terror and great delight, and went to tell his disciples. [9]Suddenly, there was Jesus himself. He met them and said, 'Greetings!' They came up to him and took hold of his feet, prostrating themselves in front of him.

[10]'Don't be afraid,' said Jesus to them. 'Go and tell my brothers that I'm going off to Galilee. Tell them they'll see me there.'

Earthquakes, angels, women running to and fro, a strange command. A highly unlikely tale. Yes, indeed, and that's the point. Nobody thought in the first century, and nobody should think now, that the point of the Easter story is that this is quite a reasonable thing to happen, that dead people really do rise if only we had the wit to see it, that it should be quite easy to believe it if only you thought about it for a few minutes.

No. It was always a strange, crazy, wild story. What else would you expect if, after all, the ancient dream of Israel was true? If the God who made the world had finally acted to turn things around, to take all the forces of chaos, pride, greed, darkness and death and allow them to do their worst, exhausting themselves in the process? If Jesus of Nazareth really was, as the centurion (greatly to his own surprise, no doubt) found himself saying three days before, 'the Son of God'? What else would you expect? A calm restatement of some philosophical truths for sage old greybeards to ponder – or events which blew the world apart and put it back in a new way?

The unlikeliest bit of the story is the bit that really does show they weren't making it up. Women were not regarded as reliable witnesses in a court of law in those days, and everybody knew it. Even the early church, where women played an important part, formulated the first official statement of resurrection faith in such a way that the women were quietly removed from the story (1 Corinthians 15.3–9). It is a thousand per cent more likely that the women were in the story at the start and then airbrushed out, rather than that they were never there in the earliest forms of the story and then inserted, in different ways, by Matthew, Mark, Luke and John. How to ruin a good story for public use! Everyone would surely say, and many sceptics did indeed say, 'How can you believe a crazy tale on the evidence of a few hysterical women?'

But, as Paul put it elsewhere in that same letter, God chooses what is weak in the world, what the world counts as foolishness, to put to shame the power and wisdom of the world. That is part of what Easter is all about. God is doing a new thing, and, as Jesus said earlier in the story, the first shall be last and the last first. Easter is a day to put everything upside down and inside out. Maybe we should have Easter processions with the young, the weak and the stranger in pride of place, letting the normal leaders sink into oblivion somewhere. Maybe we should let the children's band lead the worship and send the professional choirs into the congregation for the day. Maybe the women should lead the entire service and then, at a certain point, go and tell the men that it's time they joined in. Giving the women pride of place in the story makes exactly that point. Instead of the men getting the message and then solemnly informing the women later on, the women are in on the action from the start. It is they who have to go and tell Jesus' 'brothers' (verse 10).

But the main thing is that, once more, they are told not to be afraid (verse 5). What is there to be afraid of, if Easter has dealt with the greatest monster of all, death itself? Why should you be afraid of anything, if Jesus has been raised from the dead, if the old world has cracked open and a new world has been born?

And Easter always looks outwards. From the very start, the news that Jesus is risen contains a command: 'Go!' Go, first to Galilee; go back to where it began, back to your roots to meet the risen Jesus there and watch him transform everything, including your oldest memories. And, as you obey the command of the angel, Jesus himself may perhaps meet you in person (verse 9). Take hold of him. Worship him. This is his day, the Day of Days. Make it yours too.

Today

We praise you, Lord Jesus Christ, because you have overcome death, and opened God's new creation to all believers.

EASTER MONDAY

Matthew 28.11–15

[11]While the women were on their way, some of the soldiers who had been on guard went into the city and told the chief priests everything that had happened. [12]They called an emergency meeting with the elders, allotted a substantial sum of money, and gave it to the soldiers.

[13]'This', they told them, 'is what you are to say: "His disciples came in the night, while we were asleep, and stole him away." [14]And if this gets reported to the governor, we'll explain it to him and make sure you stay out of trouble.'

[15]They took the money and did as they had been instructed. And this story still goes the rounds among the Jews to this day.

One of the things people have often said about the early Christians' belief in Jesus' resurrection is that they were obviously so devastated by the failure of their dreams and hopes that they found a way of saying it was all right after all. A grand-sounding phrase has been developed to describe this: 'cognitive dissonance', the clash between something you have passionately believed and something which now turns out to be true. They jangle against one another, like badly played musical notes, and eventually people find a way of bringing them back into harmony. That way they don't have to adjust their original beliefs. Much easier that way.

Part of the answer to this is that the early Christians certainly weren't expecting anything like Jesus' resurrection. It wasn't part of the game plan. 'Resurrection' was something that would happen to everyone at the end, not to one person in the middle of history. They wanted Jesus to be 'king of the Jews' in the fairly ordinary sense; look at James and John and their request in chapter 20. They weren't expecting Jesus to die, especially to be crucified. They were not twiddling their thumbs on Holy Saturday saying, 'Well, that was very nasty, but of course he'll be back tomorrow.' If they were going to make up stories to explain that Jesus' project would somehow go ahead, they would have done what other Jewish groups of their day did when their leaders were killed. They would find themselves another leader, perhaps from the same family. In fact, Jesus' own brother James became the great leader of the Jerusalem church for the next 30 years. But nobody said James was the Messiah.

But the other part of the answer to what the sceptics have said is that it is in fact the sceptics, from that day to this, who are guilty of the very thing of which they are accusing the Christians. It is the sceptical world-view that has been blown apart by Jesus' resurrection. Ever since that day they have been only too eager to find stories to tell to show that actually it didn't happen, that their original world-view (in which dead people cannot, do not and will not rise again) was correct after all, that some other story will explain it. You can feel the sigh of relief in the sceptical camp each time one of these stories is put forward, however unlikely it may be. Phew! We don't need to believe that Jesus rose again. That's all right then. We can cope with him as a great teacher (with whom we may from time to time disagree). We can even see his death as a great example of love in action. We can share his vision of a world in which people live at peace. Only don't ask us to accept that he rose from the dead. That's just too much.

This reaction of the sceptics to the news of the empty tomb began very early, as we find here. Look at the way all the different parties are involved. The guards tell the priests. The priests tell the elders. Together they bribe the soldiers. They agree to tell the governor their new story. Phew! That's all right. We can continue with business as usual. Life as before – in which we run the world, we call the shots, we are the people in power. Al Gore, the former US Vice President, wrote about the ecological crisis under the title *An Inconvenient Truth*. That's as may be. The biggest inconvenient truth of all – inconvenient not just for a 'modern world-view' but for all people in positions of power and responsibility – is the belief that Jesus of Nazareth rose from the dead. Large sums of money change hands, then and now, to make sure the rumour is squashed. But it's all in vain. The best answer to the sceptics is the fact that there is now a community of people who not only say Jesus was raised from the dead. They show it by their own lives.

146

Today

Sovereign Lord, help us to meet the scorn of unbelievers with the evidence, in what we do and who we are, that you are indeed alive.

EASTER TUESDAY
Matthew 28.16–20

[16]So the eleven disciples went off to Galilee, to the mountain where Jesus had instructed them to go. [17]There they saw him, and worshipped him, though some hesitated.

[18]Jesus came towards them and addressed them.

'All authority in heaven and on earth', he said, 'has been given to me! [19]So you must go and make all the nations into disciples. Baptize them in the name of the father, and of the son, and of the holy spirit. [20]Teach them to observe everything I have commanded you. And look: I am with you, every single day, to the very end of the age.'

All four gospels tell a story which many in today's world have forgotten, or have never even known. It is the story of *how Jesus became the king of the world.* That's where we have been going, ever since, back near the beginning, Jesus came into Galilee announcing that 'heaven's kingdom is at hand'. So often this has been turned into a very different message, about 'telling people how to go to heaven', that we have ignored the far more startling truth that Jesus was actually talking about how heaven was coming to us. In other words, how God, the God of heaven and earth, was coming to earth to establish his sovereign, saving rule.

Now, risen from the dead, Jesus declares that it's happened. 'All authority in heaven and on earth has been given to me!' In other words, the prophetic picture in Daniel 7, which Jesus quoted in 24.30 and 26.64, has come true. Jesus has been exalted to be God's right-hand man. All that God now does, in heaven and on earth, he will do in and through Jesus. (Within a generation, early Christian theologians like Paul, John and the author of Hebrews would point out that this is because Jesus, long before he became human, was God's right-hand person in making the world in the first place.) This is the great message of the whole gospel. Jesus is King and Lord, not just 'in heaven' (that would be quite a 'safe' idea) but on earth as well.

But what – what on earth, we might say – does that actually mean? If Jesus is really King and Lord, why is the world still in such a mess? How does he exercise this 'lordship'? How does this sovereignty, claimed so strongly in this passage, work out on the ground?

The whole gospel, once more, is written in order to give the answer to that. Again, it's an answer many people today have not even begun to think through. Ask yourself this question: how did Jesus come to this point of being king? The answer is obvious. He didn't do it in the way the disciples expected, in the way the crowds wanted, in the way which the chief priests and Pilate assumed he would behave. He didn't follow the normal human path to power, pushing and shoving his way forward, fighting and killing until his position was established. He came as the Servant, the one who took people's infirmities and diseases on to himself, the one who suffered insults and mocking and torture and death. He was obedient, throughout his life, to a different vision of power, a different sort of kingdom-dream. And his resurrection not only showed that he was right. It established his kingdom, his *type of* kingdom, once and for all.

But if that's the sort of kingdom it is, it must be put into operation, not by his followers bullying and harrying and forcing the rest of the world to come into line. That's what people are afraid of today when they warn against 'theocracy', a rule-of-God which would quickly turn into the bossy, self-righteous 'rule' of those who claim to speak for God.

Sometimes, indeed, the church has behaved in exactly that way. But that is a denial of the Lord they claim to worship. Jesus' followers are to implement his kingdom by *going and making disciples*, learners, students, followers who will be shaped by Jesus' example and teaching. They are to 'baptize' them, plunging them into the very name and life and character of the true God, who is Father, Son and Spirit. They are to teach them everything Jesus commanded, particularly all those wonderful words in the Sermon on the Mount about the meek inheriting the earth, about a different way to be human. That is the character of Jesus' rule, and that is the means by which that rule will be established.

We live at a time of great transition and turbulence in our society. Dreams of 'progress' and 'enlightenment' seem to have produced the exact opposite. Supposedly civilized society has gone back to the use of torture. Supposedly grown-up society cannot educate the rising generation in anything but trivia. This same society regularly tells the church that it is on the way out. The Christian message is bad for you, they say; it's out of date, it's disproved.

This is ridiculous. There is every reason to hope that this year, or this decade, or this century, God will do new things. Jesus is still Lord – but he rules in the same way that he lived, taught and died. When his followers learn again to do the same, we shall see a fresh start. And the encouragement we need is found in the final words of Matthew's gospel, picking up neatly the promise made to Joseph at the very beginning. His name will be 'Emmanuel', said the angel, which means 'God with us'. That God-with-us promise, that heaven-on-earth assurance, has come true in Jesus. Millions of Christians know this in their daily experience, their praying, their living, their work for his kingdom. 'I am with you always, to the end of the age.' That is a promise you can stake your life on. It is also a challenge: if *Jesus himself* is 'with you', what should you be doing? How then should you live? Easter is a time to ask precisely that sort of question. It is also a time to discover God's powerful answer.

Today

Risen Lord Jesus, be with us as you have promised, and help us to go into all the world to bring all nations under the rule of your love.

EASTER WEDNESDAY
Matthew 2.1–12

[1]When Jesus was born, in Bethlehem of Judaea, at the time when Herod was king, some wise and learned men came to Jerusalem from the East.

[2]'Where is the one,' they asked, 'who has been born to be king of the Jews? We have seen his star in the east, and we have come to worship him.'

[3]When King Herod heard this, he was very disturbed, and the whole of Jerusalem was as well. [4]He called together all the chief priests and scribes of the people, and enquired from them where the Messiah was to be born.

[5]'In Bethlehem of Judaea,' they replied. 'That's what it says in the prophet:

[6]You, Bethlehem, in Judah's land
are not the least of Judah's princes;
from out of you will come the ruler
who will shepherd Israel my people.'

[7]Then Herod called the wise men to him in secret. He found out from them precisely when the star had appeared. [8]Then he sent them to Bethlehem.

'Off you go,' he said, 'and make a thorough search for the child. When you find him, report back to me, so that I can come and worship him too.'

[9]When they heard what the king said, they set off. There was the star, the one they had seen in the east, going ahead of

them! It went and stood still over the place where the child was. [10]When they saw the star, they were beside themselves with joy and excitement. [11]They went into the house and saw the child, with Mary his mother, and they fell down and worshipped him. They opened their treasure-chests, and gave him presents: gold, frankincense and myrrh.

[12]They were warned in a dream not to go back to Herod. So they returned to their own country by a different route.

We are now going to do something rather different. We have followed the story which Matthew tells, the story of Jesus from before his birth to after his resurrection. But Matthew was of course writing for Christians who already knew more or less 'what happened'. They were already people who believed in Jesus, that he had died to rescue them from sin and death, that he had been raised again and was now the world's true Lord. How would they then read Matthew's gospel, not just as a faithful account of what had happened in the past, but as a blueprint and set of clues for how they should be living as followers of this risen Jesus today?

I have chosen four passages that we haven't looked at in detail earlier in the book, to take us forward from the Easter story itself into the much longer Easter story that continues to this day. Jesus' Easter people – you and me, in other words – now read the gospels in order to discover, again and again, the presence and power and leading of Jesus in and through our lives and witness. And we begin with that wonderful story about the three wise men.

Here, Matthew is saying, Jesus was already mysteriously revealed as 'Lord of the world' – even though the present Jewish ruler, the sad and bad old king Herod, had no interest in such things except to kill enough people (in this case, little babies) to make sure nobody would upset his own shaky grip on power. Wise men from the East: we are not told here that they were 'kings', though later legend has seen them as such.

Certainly Matthew intends them as representatives of the 'many who will come from east and west' to share the ancient Jewish dream of God's kingdom, and all because of Jesus (see 8.11). By the same token, he is seeing Herod as typical of those 'sons of the kingdom' who will, at the same time, miss out on the promise. As John the Baptist would say in the next chapter, God can raise up 'children of Abraham' from these stones (3.9).

The story of the three wise men, then, can be seen in the light of Easter as a great encouragement to the little church as it sets off on its mission to the wider world: the wider world has already heard about him and begun to come looking for him! But here there is a delicate balance to be kept. Some, eager to show how much God loves the whole world, have seen all non-Jewish religions and philosophies as equally valid, merely needing to be encouraged and developed. But that's not how the story works.

The wisdom of the East, including the stargazing which was such a major part of ancient learning, had brought the wise men to the point where they were ready to travel to the land of the Jews to find the new king. But they needed help to find the right spot. Help was at hand in the form of the Jewish scriptures. They and they alone provided the clue to Bethlehem. Without them, the wise men had simply ended up at the wrong address – a dangerous place to be, as anyone in Herod's court could have told them. But, with great irony, the chief priests and scribes who have told the travellers where to find the royal child have no interest in going themselves to see whether it's true. They assume it isn't – until, later, Herod smells a rat and sends in his thugs to kill the babies.

Matthew seems to be saying, to his resurrection-based church, that their mission will remain rooted in the Jewish scriptures, and that they will be able with their help to draw the wisdom of the world into homage to the world's rightful king. But he is also warning them that they must not expect all the Jewish people to join in. As Paul would put it, God has subjected all people to disobedience, so that he might have mercy on all. The good news of Jesus, his kingdom-message, cross and resurrection, is always humbling to all people. It is the place where the scriptures and the wisdom of the world can meet and celebrate, but it will take something more as well. The 'wise men' could just as well have been called 'the humble men', or indeed 'the obedient men'. It's people like that who could then be called 'the overwhelmed-with-joy' people.

Today

Risen Lord, give us a vision of the whole world coming to worship at your feet, and enable us to play a part in bringing that to reality.

EASTER THURSDAY

Matthew 6.25–34

[25]'So let me tell you: don't worry about your life – what to eat, what to drink; don't worry about your body – what to wear. There's more to life than food! There's more to the body than a suit of clothes! [26]Have a good look at the birds in the sky. They don't plant seeds, they don't bring in the harvest, they don't store things in barns – and your father in heaven feeds them! Think how different you are from them! [27]Can any of you add fifteen inches to your height just by worrying about it?

[28]'And why worry about what to wear? Take a tip from the lilies in the countryside. They don't work; they don't weave; [29]but, let me tell you, not even Solomon in all his finery was dressed as well as one of these. [30]So if God gives that sort of clothing even to the grass in the field, which is here today and on the bonfire tomorrow, isn't he going to clothe you too, you little-faith lot?

[31]'So don't worry away with your "What'll we eat?" and "What'll we drink?" and "What'll we wear?" [32]Those are all

153

the kinds of things the Gentiles fuss about, and your heavenly father knows you need them all. [33]Instead, make your top priority God's kingdom and his way of life, and all these things will be given to you as well.

[34]'So don't worry about tomorrow. Tomorrow can worry about itself. One day's trouble at a time is quite enough.'

Now, in Easter week, try reading the whole Sermon on the Mount as a blueprint for how Jesus' Easter-people should live. Now at last, with Jesus leading the way through death to new life, we see what it might mean to be poor in spirit, to be meek, peacemakers, and so on. Now, already, the mourners are being comforted, the pure in heart glimpsing the living God in Jesus himself. Now at last, as well, those who follow Jesus will be persecuted because of their love for him and the new world of justice and joy which he has opened up, which challenges the old world to its core. Now, at last, we can see the sense in the demanding new way of life which he has launched.

That is the spirit in which, for instance, we should read the bracing commands of 5.21–48. This is what it might mean to be genuinely human! The Easter message declares that it is possible to live without anger, without lust, without divorce, swearing, revenge and hatred. Most of the world doesn't know this, but Jesus knew it; and at Easter he calls us to die to all those things, and come alive to his new way of life. Yes, it will be tough. Yes, dying in any sense is hard and unpleasant. So many theories about human behaviour have assumed that we ought to feel as comfortable as possible as much as possible. Then we wonder why life goes downhill, rather than attaining the heights we glimpse from time to time. Easter is where we not only see those heights but start to scale them.

Then, as the Sermon reaches a kind of climax, we have this passage about worry – or rather, about not worrying. Modern life, of course, thrives on worry. We only have to think back a century or two before radio, television, regular swift mail around the country and the world, and so on, to realize that for most people most of the time the world beyond their immediate village was a closed book. Worry was localized – none the easier for that, but think what we have done. We have made a global issue of it: we worry about nuclear power in the Middle East, about bush fires in Australia, about ecological disasters in Alaska. And, of course, this doesn't remove the local and personal worries about meeting the bills, about feeding the family, about the uncertainty of life itself.

And Jesus tells us – the Easter Jesus tells us – not to worry about any of them. He could give that instruction already, during his ministry; how much more can he give it now that he is raised from the dead, now that he has overthrown the greatest worry of all, death itself? One of the chief notes in the life of the early Christians was joy: joy because a new way of life had been launched, new creation had begun, and it was clear that God had commenced his reign and could be trusted to bring it to completion. 'Seek first the kingdom of God, and his righteousness,' said Jesus, 'and all these things will be given to you as well.' And Easter reaffirms, gloriously, the way in which Jesus drew his examples from the natural order. The birds don't plant seed and reap harvests, but they get enough to eat. The lilies don't work at weaving, yet they are dressed magnificently. Other philosophies might scoff at such examples: they come from this world of space, time and matter, not the eternal world of ideas. But Easter reminds us emphatically that the world of space, time and matter is *redeemed*, not abandoned. In raising Jesus, God has reaffirmed the goodness of the natural world, and his compassionate care for it. In that care we can rest secure.

Worry and Easter, then, don't go together. Someone once asked that great teacher and saint, Bishop Lesslie Newbigin, whether he was an optimist or a pessimist. 'I am neither an optimist', he said, 'nor a pessimist. Jesus Christ is risen from the dead!' He had learned the Easter lesson which brings the Sermon on the Mount to life. Our life.

Today

Help us, gracious Lord, to live our whole life in full and joyful trust in the power of your resurrection.

EASTER FRIDAY

Matthew 13.1–23

[1]That very day Jesus went out of the house and sat down beside the sea. [2]Large crowds gathered around him, so he got into a boat and sat down. The whole crowd was standing on the shore.

[3]He had much to say to them, and he said it all in parables.

'Listen!' he said. 'Once there was a sower who went out to sow. [4]As he sowed, some seed fell beside the path, and the birds came and ate it up. [5]Some seed fell on rocky soil, where it didn't have much earth. It sprang up at once because it didn't have depth of soil. [6]But when the sun was high it got scorched, and it withered because it didn't have any root. [7]Other seed fell in among thorns, and the thorns grew up and choked it. [8]And other seed fell into good soil, and produced a crop, some a hundred times over, some sixty, and some thirty times over. [9]If you've got ears, then listen!'

[10]His disciples came to him.

'Why are you speaking to them in parables?' they asked.

[11]'You've been given the gift of knowing the secrets of the kingdom of heaven,' he replied, 'but they haven't been given it. [12]Anyone who already has something will be given more, and they will have plenty. But anyone who has nothing – even what they have will be taken away! [13]That's why I speak to them in parables, so that they may look but not see, and hear but not understand or take it in. [14]Isaiah's prophecy is coming true in them:

You will listen and listen but won't understand,
You will look and look but not see.
[15]This people's heart has gone flabby and fat,
Their ears are muffled and dull,
So they won't be able to see with their eyes,
Or hear with their ears, or know in their heart,
And they won't turn again and be healed.

[16]But there's great news for *your* eyes: they can see! And for your ears: they can hear! [17]I'm telling you the truth: many prophets and holy people longed to see what you see and didn't see it, and to hear what you hear and didn't hear it.'

[18]'All right, then,' Jesus continued, 'this is what the sower story is all about. [19]When someone hears the word of the kingdom and doesn't understand it, the evil one comes and snatches away what was sown in their heart. This corresponds to what was sown beside the path. [20]What was sown on rocky ground is the person who hears the word and immediately receives it with delight, [21]but doesn't have any root of their own. Someone like that only lasts a short time; as soon as there's any trouble or persecution because of the word, they trip up at once. [22]The one sown among thorns is the one who hears the word, but the world's worries and the seduction of wealth choke the word and it doesn't bear fruit. [23]But the one sown on good soil is the one who hears the word and understands it. Someone like that will bear fruit: one will produce a hundred times over, another sixty, and another thirty times over.'

Reading Jesus' parables in Easter week is particularly fruit-ful. Imagine Matthew's friends reading his book, with their own Easter celebrations now a regular weekly feature of life, and hearing them in a whole new way. Jesus had spoken elsewhere, after all, about his own life in terms of a grain of seed falling into the earth and dying, and then bearing a great deal of fruit. It looks as though he was applying to himself the strange picture in the parable of the Sower, where much seed seems to be thrown away (how sad, people sometimes say, that Jesus died so young when he had so much still to give! What a waste!), and yet some bears fruit 30, 60 or 100 times over.

What started life, then, as Jesus' explanation of how his own kingdom-work was going ahead during the course of his public career can be translated, without difficulty, into the explanation that the Easter church now needs for how the work of world mission will fare. One of the standard objections to the Christian message, as we saw, goes like this: how can you say the kingdom of heaven has arrived on earth, when it's obvious, looking around you, that nothing of the kind has happened? Things are still pretty bleak. Often Jesus' followers seem to be part of the problem, not part of the solution.

Jesus' own explanation of how the kingdom works is still the classic answer to this question. What did you expect: that God would send in the tanks like a totalitarian dictator, crush the opposition and set up a 'kingdom' which would leave half the world bruised and resentful? What sort of a 'god' would that be? No! God will bring in his kingdom by the same means, the same strange process, that he seems to use in the natural world. Seeds will be sown; many will apparently be lost, but others will be powerfully fruitful. Or, as the chapter goes on, there will be seeds sown which are then threatened by weeds. One day the weeds will be pulled up, but for the moment they grow side by side. Or again, the kingdom will come like seed growing secretly. At the moment there may be nothing to see, but suddenly, one day, people will be putting in the sickle because it's harvest time. In other words: yes, the kingdom has indeed been launched; yes, it is making its way in the world; but no, it isn't doing so in the way you might have imagined. It is doing so in the way God has imagined: by the Sower himself becoming the seed sown in good soil, and rising again to celebrate the harvest of God's new creation.

Today

Give us the faith, good Lord, to see your kingdom at work even when seeds seem wasted and the soil seems bare. Thank you for the promise of the great harvest, of which your resurrection was the first fruits.

EASTER SATURDAY

Matthew 22.34–40

³⁴When the Pharisees heard that Jesus had silenced the Sadducees, they got together in a group. ³⁵One of them, a lawyer, put him on the spot with this question.

³⁶'Teacher,' he said, 'which is the most important commandment in the law?'

³⁷'You must love the Lord your God', replied Jesus, 'with all your heart, with all your life, and with all your strength. ³⁸This is the first commandment, and it's the one that really matters. ³⁹The second is similar, and it's this: You must love your neighbour as yourself. ⁴⁰The entire law consists of footnotes to these two commandments – and that goes for the prophets, too.'

'So what's your all-time favourite song, then?'

I listened as John put his friend on the spot. They had been discussing music of various sorts and styles. This was a way of getting to the heart of the matter.

'Let me play safe,' the friend replied. 'I'm not going for something new. I'll stick with "Yesterday", by Paul McCartney.'

John was shocked. 'I thought it would be something by Schubert,' he complained. 'You're always on about him.'

'Yes, I know,' came the reply. 'But actually I think "Yesterday" draws together the whole tradition of earlier song, and says so much in a short space. It's beautiful, and it's packed full of meaning.'

The debate will go on. Some readers will no doubt be as shocked as John was. But the explanation was a good one. We're not talking about a whim here, a sudden passing fancy. We're talking about something that draws a much larger picture together and holds it there.

Questions like this come in many shapes and sizes. What's the best golf course in the world? Which is the finest Shakespeare play? Which Scottish mountain gives you the best walk? But one of the most famous, a question repeated in various forms throughout Jewish literature, is the one the Pharisees asked Jesus: 'Which commandment in the law is the greatest?'

Now we note that this isn't simply a question about the relative importance of the commands against stealing, murder, adultery and so on. The law – Israel's Torah – was not just a list of rules to make life a bit less unpleasant. It was the God-given blueprint for the national life, the life that would make Israel the light of the world. It was, so many Jews believed, a direct revelation from God himself, thus making the Torah almost divine in itself. And part of the point of Torah, for the Pharisees of the time, was that any Jew, anywhere in the world, could follow it. Most Jews couldn't get to the Temple in Jerusalem except at the most once or twice in a lifetime. Any Jew could study, learn and follow Torah.

Jesus' answer to the question was straight down the line. 'Love God with all your heart, soul and mind,' he said, 'and love your neighbour as yourself.' As far as it went, as an answer to the question of the time, it was beyond reproach. These are central to the Old Testament as well as the New, and contain within them pretty much everything else the law prescribes.

But what happens if we read them in the light of Easter?

We suddenly discover that something Matthew has often hinted at comes true in a new way. Jesus came not to abolish the law, but to fulfil it. But how did he fulfil it? Not by laboriously obeying all the biblical commands, one by one, ticking them off on a mental list. Rather, by doing and being all that Israel was called to do and be. He became the defining point, the blueprint and yardstick, for the people of God. In his death on the cross he offered God the full love, obedience and devotion of heart, mind and soul to which Israel had been called. And in that same death he reached out in love to neighbours far and near, to the whole world for whom he was dying. He became not just the teacher of a new, fulfilled Torah. He was the fulfilled Torah in person.

The resurrection of Jesus therefore declares that the law, as summed up here, has been fulfilled to the uttermost – by Jesus himself. And, precisely because of the resurrection, it can be fulfilled anywhere and everywhere. Followers of Jesus don't need to go to the Temple in Jerusalem. They can go to Jesus, which is what they do whenever they love God with heart, mind and soul, and their neighbours as themselves.

And when people say, as they will, that these things are very difficult, then Jesus is on hand, with them always to the close of the age, to explain that the more they look at him and learn from him, the more they will discover what it means to love God, and the more energy and goodwill they will find welling up inside themselves to love their neighbours as well. Jesus' resurrection is the greatest demonstration of the love of God for his whole creation, evoking in us an answering love. And when we glimpse God's new world, in which all are invited to share, we look upon our neighbours, of all shapes, sorts and sizes, with new eyes. These are people for whom Jesus died. These are people we shall learn to love as we love ourselves.

This is what it means to be genuinely human. Easter offers us the direct route to be the people we were made to be. God's people. Jesus' people. People of love.

Today

Gracious Lord Jesus, dying for us and rising again: show us more and more how great the Father's love is for us, so that we may be drawn to love him more and more in return; and show us, for his sake and yours, how to love our neighbours as we love ourselves.